THE Crossword Puzzler's Handbook

CIDER MILL PRESS

BOOK PUBLISHERS

Kennebunkport, Maine

THE Crossword Puzzler's Handbook

1000 PEOPLE PLACES AND THINGS YOU NEED TO KNOW TO SOLVE CROSSWORD PUZZLES!

Compiled by Richard Showstack

13-Digit ISBN: 978-1-60433-022-9
10-Digit ISBN: 1-60433-022-8

This book may be ordered by mail from the publisher. Please include $2.50 for postage and handling.

Please support your local bookseller first!

Books published by Cider Mill Press Book Publishers are available at special discounts for bulk purchases in the United States by corporations, institutions, and other organizations. For more information, please contact the publisher.

Cider Mill Press Book Publishers
"Where good books are ready for press"
12 Port Farm Road
Kennebunkport, Maine 04046
Visit us on the web!
www.cidermillpress.com

Design by Ponderosa Pine Design, Vicky Vaughn Shea
Typography: Alons Antique, Amasis, Farao, Secret Service

Printed in China

1 2 3 4 5 6 7 8 9 0

First Edition

Contents

To all my fellow
crazy, wild, passionate,
fanatical, lunatic, nutty
cruciverbalists
everywhere!

Introduction

This book is not a dictionary. Rather, it is a compilation of "cross weirds" (words that appear in crossword puzzles more often than in general conversation or the media).

It is does not include the simple words that often appear in crosswords—ones that the reader/solver no doubt already knows. Nor does it include the difficult or sesquipedalian (having many syllables; long) words that only a few people know (or want to know).

It includes those "in-between words" that are not commonly used but, because they use the most common letters of the alphabet, often appear in crosswords.

There are two ways to use this collection: You may use it as a reference when you come upon a crossword clue that rings a bell but you just cannot remember the word. Or you may use it as a study guide, both to improve your crossword-solving skills as well as your general vocabulary.

Whichever way you use it, have fun!

PART ONE

PEOPLE AND OTHER LIVING THINGS

Actors/Actresses/Comedians/ Directors/Performers

Anouk Aimée: A French actress (b. 1932), best known for her appearance in *Un Homme et Une Femme* [*A Man and a Woman*], 1966.

Adele Astaire: An American dancer and entertainer (1896–1981) (and Fred Astaire's elder sister).

Ang Lee: Chinese director (b. 1954) who won the Academy Award for Best Director for *Brokeback Mountain*.

Arte Johnson: Comic actor (b. 1929), best known for appearing on *Rowan and Martin's Laugh-In*.

Ava Gardner: An American actress (b. 1922), sex symbol of the 1940s and 1950s.

Cheri Oteri: An American actress (b. 1965), debuted on *Saturday Night Live* in 1995.

Diana Rigg: A British actress (b. 1938), known for appearing in the TV show, *The Avengers* (1965–1968).

Ed Asner: An American actor (b. 1929), best known for portraying Lou Grant on *The Mary Tyler Moore*

Show (1970–1974) and for winning an Emmy for his appearance in *Roots* (1977).

Elia Kazan: A director born (1909-2003) to Greek parents in Turkey, directed (among other films) *Gentleman's Agreement* (1947), *A Streetcar Named Desire* (1951), *On the Waterfront* (1954), *East of Eden* (1955), *Splendor in the Grass* (1961), and *America, America* (1963).

Elke Sommer: A German actress (b. 1940), a sex symbol in the 1960s, appeared in *A Shot in the Dark* (1964) with Peter Sellers.

Emil Jannings: A European actor (1884–1950), the first winner of the Academy Award (in 1928) for Best Actor (for *The Way of All Flesh* and *The Last Command*).

Emo Philips: An American comedian (b. 1956).

Erik Estrada: An American actor (b. 1949), best known for a lead role in the TV series *Chips* (1977–1983).

Esai Morales: An American actor (b. 1962), appeared in *La Bamba* (the biopic of Ritchie Valens) (1987) and *NYPD Blue*.

Eva Gabor: A British-Hungarian actress (1919–1995), sister of Zsa Zsa Gabor. Best known for her role in the TV sitcom, *Green Acres* (1965–1971).

Ezio Pinza: An Italian opera singer (1892–1957), appeared in the movie version of *South Pacific* (1949).

Gena Rowlands: An American actress (b. 1930), married to John Cassavetes (1954–1989).

Ida Lupino: An English film actress and director (1918–1995).

Ilona Massey: A Hungarian actress (1912–1974).

Iman: A supermodel (born in Somalia in 1955), married to British actor and rock star David Bowie.

Inga Swenson: An American actress (b. 1932), best known for her portrayal of the German cook on the TV sitcom *Benson*.

Ione Skye: A British actress (b. 1971), appeared in *Say Anything, River's Edge*, and *The Rachel Papers*.

Jack Elam: An American western film actor (1918–2003).

Jacques Tati: A French film director and actor (1908–1982).

Joanne Dru: An American film actress (1922–1996).

Lana Turner: An American actress (1921–1955).

Len Cariou: A Canadian actor (b. 1939).

Lena Olin: A Swedish actress (b. 1955), appeared in several of Ingmar Bergman's films, as well as *The Unbearable Lightness of Being* and *Enemies: A Love Story* and the TV series, *Alias*.

Lina Wertmüller: A European actress (b. 1926), best known as director of *Swept Away* and *Seven Beauties*.

Mako: A Japanese-American actor (1933–2006).

Mamie Van Doren: An American actress (1908–1992), best known as a sex symbol in the 1950s.

Maryam D'Abo: An English actress (b. 1960). (Second cousin of Olivia D'Abo)

Milo O'Shea: An Irish actor (b. 1926).

Moira Shearer: A Scottish ballet dancer and actress (1926–2006).

Nia Peeples: An American singer and actress (b. 1961).

Nita Naldi: A silent film actress (1897–1961).

Olivia D'Abo: An English actress (b. 1969). (Second cousin of Maryam D'Abo)

Patricia Neal: An American actress (b. 1926). Won the Academy Award for Best Actress in 1963 for her appearance in *Hud* (with Paul Newman).

Pola Negri: A Polish silent film actress (1894–1987).

Rene Auberjonois: An American actor (b. 1940). Portrayed the character Odo in *Star Trek: Deep Space Nine*.

Robert Urich: An American actor (1946–2002), best known for playing private investigators on the TV series *Vega$* (1978–1981) and *Spenser: For Hire* (1985–1988).

Ruby Dee: An African-American actress (b. 1924), long married to actor Ossie Davis.

Ruby Keeler: An American actress, singer, and (tap) dancer (1909–1993).

Ron Ely: An American actor (b. 1938), best known for starring in the TV series *Tarzan* in the 1960s.

Rona Barrett: An American gossip columnist (b. 1936).

Roone Arledge: An American sports broadcasting pioneer (1931–2002) who was chairman of ABC News from 1977 until his death.

Sada Thompson: An American actress (b. 1929), best known for her role in the TV series, *Family.*

Sandra Dee: An American film actress (1942–2005), best known for her role as Gidget.

Sela Ward: An American actress (b. 1956), best known for her roles on the TV series *Sisters* and *Once and Again.*

Shari Lewis: An American ventriloquist, puppeteer, and children's TV host (1933–1998), best known for her puppet Lamb Chop.

Susan Dey: An American actress (b. 1952), best known for her roles on *The Partridge Family* and *L.A. Law.*

Theda Bara: A silent film actress (1885–1955).

Twyla Tharp: An American dancer and choreographer (b. 1941).

Tyne Daly: An American stage and screen actress (b. 1946).

Uta Hagen: German-born American actress and acting teacher (1919–2004).

Animals/Birds/Fish/Insects

Aardvark: A nocturnal mammal, native to Africa, that feeds almost exclusively on ants and termites.

Adder: A small terrestrial venomous snake.

Aedes: The genus of a mosquito, originally found in the tropics, that transmits deadly diseases.

Ameba/Amoeba: A genus of protozoa.

Ani: A New World bird related to the cuckoos.

Asp: An archaic name for a number of species of poisonous snakes (often mentioned in the context that Cleopatra committed suicide by allowing herself to be bitten by an asp).

Brant: A small goose.

Calico: A blotchy or spotted animal; especially a domestic cat that is mainly white but has red and black patches.

Carapace: A section of the exoskeleton or shell of a number of animals (such as crustaceans and turtles/tortoises).

Coati: A small tropical mammal, related to the raccoon.

Coho: A type of salmon.

Conger: A marine eel, native to the Atlantic Ocean.

Corgi: A Welsh breed of dog.

Daw: Short for "jackdaw," a small bird related to crows and ravens.

Drake: A male duck.

Dugong: A herbivorous marine mammal native to tropical coastal waters, similar to a "sea cow."

Eft: A newt; especially, the terrestrial phase of a predominantly aquatic newt.

Eider: A large northern sea duck whose fine soft down ("eiderdown") is used in clothing.

Eland: A large African antelope.

Elver: A young eel.

Emmet: An ant.

Emu: An Australian flightless bird. (See: *moa, rhea, ratite*)

Enos: A chimpanzee launched into space by the U.S. in 1961.

Ern(e): A sea eagle.

Gar: A needlefish.

Ibex: A wild Old World goat.

Imago: An insect in its final adult (and typically winged) state.

Jennet/Jenny: A female donkey.

Krait: A venomous snake of South Asia.

Leveret: A very young hare.

Lobo: A gray wolf.

Mako: A kind of shark.

Merino:
1. A kind of sheep; or
2. A kind of wool, yarn, or fabric.

Merl(e): A kind of blackbird.

Midge: A tiny fly. (See: *no-see-um*)

Moa: A very large extinct flightless bird of New Zealand. (See: *emu, rhea, ratite*)

Nene: A Hawaiian goose.

No-see-um: A biting midge. (See: *midge*)

Nutria: A large South American rodent.

Okapi: An African mammal, related to the giraffe.

Onager: A wild ass of central Asia.

Opah: A brilliantly colored large fish.

Orca: A killer whale.

Oso: The Spanish word for "bear."

Ousel/Ouzel: A blackbird.

Owlet: A small or young owl.

Parr: A young salmon.

Puma: A cougar.

Quahog: A kind of clam.

Ratite: Any of a variety of flightless birds, including the ostrich. (See: *emu, moa, rhea*)

Remora: A kind of fish that uses a suction disk on its head to adhere to other fish.

Rhea: A South American flightless bird.

Roan: A horse, usually with a red coat.

Roe: The eggs of a fish or of an invertebrate.

Serin: An Old World finch related to the canary.

Shad: A herring-like fish.

Shar-pei: A dog, originating in China, with loose wrinkled skin.

Shoat: A young hog.

Sloe: The fruit of the blackthorn, used in "sloe gin."

Smew: A small Eurasian duck.

Span: A pair of animals (usually oxen) driven together.

Stoat: An ermine, especially in its brown summer coat.

Tapir: A tropical mammal with a long snout.

Tarpon: A long fish that is often caught for sport.

Tetra: A small brightly colored South American fish often bred in tropical aquariums.

Titi: A small South American monkey.

Tsetse (fly): An African fly that transmits disease (especially sleeping sickness).

Vole: A rodent that resembles a rat or mouse.

Wapiti: A type of elk.

Architects/Artists/Designers

Al Capp: An American cartoonist (1909–1979), best known for the comic strip *Li'l Abner,* about hillbillies who live in Dogpatch.

Christian Dior: A French fashion designer (1905–1957).

Diego Rivera: A Mexican painter (1886–1957), best known for his large mural paintings and for being married to Frida Kahlo.

Eero Saarinen: A Finnish-American architect (1910–1961), who designed (among other things) the Gateway Arch in St. Louis, the TWA terminal at JFK Airport, and Dulles Airport, outside of Washington, DC.

Erno Rubik: The Hungarian inventor, sculptor, and professor of architecture who invented the Rubik's Cube.

Erté: A Russian-born French artist and designer (1892–1990) whose French name (Erté) was based on the French pronunciation of the initials of his birth name (Romain de Tirtoff).

Estée Lauder: With husband Joseph Lauder, co-founded the company that is now one of the world's leading manufacturers and marketers of skin care, cosmetics, perfume, and hair care products.

Frida Kahlo: A Mexican painter (1907–1954), was married to Diego Rivera.

I. M. Pei: A Chinese-American architect who designed (among other structures) the John Hancock Tower and John F. Kennedy Library (both in Boston), the Javits Convention Center in New York City, the new pyramid-style main entrance of the Louvre Museum in Paris, and the Rock and Roll Hall of Fame in Cleveland.

Inigo Jones: The first significant English architect (1573–1652).

Jean Arp: A German-French sculptor, painter, and poet (1886–1966), best known as a founding member of the Dada movement (in 1916). (See: *Max Ernst*)

Joan Miro: A Spanish surrealist painter, sculptor, and ceramist (1893–1983).

Jose Maria Sert: A Spanish muralist.

Max Ernst: A German Dadaist and surrealist artist (1891–1976).

Mies van der Rohe: A German-born American architect (1886–1969).

Piet Mondrian: A Dutch painter (1872–1944) whose paintings consisted of straight perpendicular lines and rectangular forms.

René La Coste: A French tennis player and businessman (1904–1996), best known for his tennis shirt, which has a crocodile logo on it.

René Magritte: A Belgian surrealist artist (1898–1967) best known for his droll images.

Shel Silverstein: An American poet, songwriter, musician, composer, cartoonist, screenwriter, and author of children's books (1930–1999).

Yves St. Laurent: A French fashion designer (b. 1936). (His initials—YSL—appear in crossword puzzle answers more than his name does.)

Athletes/Coaches/Other Sports People

ALer : A player in the American [baseball] League. (See: *NLer*)

Althea Gibson: The first African-American woman (1927–2003) to be a competitor on the world tennis tour.

Ara Parseghian: The former head coach (b. 1923) of the University of Notre Dame football team (1964–1974).

Arthur Ashe: A prominent African-American tennis player (1943–1993), the first to be selected to the U.S. Davis Cup Team.

Bela Karolyi: Coach (b. 1942) of both the Romanian and U.S. Olympic gymnastic teams.

Bobby Orr: A retired Canadian ice hockey player (b. 1948).

Bud Selig: The Commissioner of Baseball (b. 1934).

Chris Evert: A former number-one woman tennis player from the U.S. (b. 1954).

Eli Manning: A quarterback for the New York Giants.

Emil Zatopek: A Czech Olympic gold medalist (1922–2000) in long distance running.

Ernie Els: A South African golfer (b. 1969).

Enos Slaughter: A baseball player (1916–2002).

Evel Knievel: American daredevil (b. 1938), best known for long-distance motorcycle jumping.

Evonne Goolagong: A former tennis player (b. 1951), from an Australian aboriginal family.

Gertrude Ederle: An American swimmer (1906–2003), the first woman to swim across the English Channel.

Hana Mandlikova: A former pro tennis player (b. 1962) from the Czech Republic.

Ilie Nastase: A former Romanian tennis player (b. 1946).

Ivan Lendl: A former Czech tennis player (b. 1960).

Mel Ott: A baseball player (1909–1958) who played for the New York Giants for his entire career.

Midori Ito: A Japanese figure skater (b. 1969).

NLer : A player in the National [baseball] League. (See: *ALer*)

Orel Hersheiser: A former baseball pitcher (b. 1958).

Pele: A former Brazilian soccer player (b. 1940).

Phil Mahre: A former American skier (b. 1957).

Robb Nen: A former baseball relief pitcher (b. 1969).

Sam Snead: An American golfer (1912–2002).

Sasha Cohen: An American figure skater (b. 1984).

Seve Ballesteros: A Spanish golfer (b. 1957).

Sonja Henie: A Norwegian figure skater and actress (1912–1969).

Tara Lipinski: An American figure skater (b. 1982).

Ty Cobb: A baseball player (1886–1961), nicknamed "The Georgia Peach."

Ute: A student (especially an athlete) at the University of Utah.

Wes Unseld: A former American basketball player (b. 1946).

Authors/Playwrights/Writers

Aesop: A Greek slave, author of *Aesop's Fables*.

Anais Nin: A French-born author (1903–1977), best known for her published diaries.

Anita Loos: An American screenwriter, playwright, and author (1888–1981), best known for the play *Gentlemen Prefer Blondes* (1925).

Ayn Rand: A Russian-born American novelist and philosopher (1905–1982), best known for her philosophy of Objectivism for writing *The Fountainhead* and *Atlas Shrugged*.

Charles Dickens: An English novelist (1812–1870), author of many famous works, including *Oliver Twist*, *A Christmas Carol*, *David Copperfield*, *A Tale of Two Cities*, and *Great Expectations*. (In crossword puzzles, reference is often made to his pen name, "Boz.")

Charles Lamb: An English essayist (1775–1834) who wrote under the pen name of "Elia."

Clifford Odets: An American playwright and screenwriter (1906–1963). His works include *Waiting for Lefty, Awake and Sing!, Golden Boy,* and *Sweet Smell of Success.*

Eda LeShan: An American children's author (1922–2002).

Edgar Allan Poe: An American poet and short story writer (1809–1849), author of "The Gold Bug," "The Pit and the Pendulum," "The Raven," "The Tell-Tale Heart," "The Murders in the Rue Morgue," and "The Fall of the House of Usher." Died in Baltimore. (His initials "EAP" often appear as a crossword answer.)

Emile Zola: A French novelist (1840–1902), whose work reflected "Naturalism." His 1898 letter, *J'accuse*" publicly accused the French government of anti-Semitism and of wrongly placing Alfred Dreyfus (a French military officer) in jail.

Enid Bagnold: A British author and playwright (1889–1981), best known for writing *National Velvet.*

Erle Stanley Gardner: An American author of detective stories (1889–1970), best known as the creator of the character "Perry Mason."

Eugene Ionesco: A French-Romanian playwright and dramatist (1909–1994) of the "Theatre of the Absurd," best known for his play, *Rhinoceros.*

Evan Hunter: An American author and screenwriter (1926–2005), perhaps even better known under his pen name, "Ed McBain."

Ezra Pound: An American poet (1885–1972) who became an expatriate in Paris and then Italy, best known for *The Cantos*.

Gay Talese: An American author (b. 1932) who wrote (among other books) *Thy Neighbor's Wife*.

Henrik Ibsen: A Norwegian playwright (1828–1906) who wrote *Peer Gynt*, *A Doll's House*, *Ghosts* and *Hedda Gabler*.

Herman Hesse: A German-born writer (1877–1962) who wrote *Siddhartha* and *Steppenwolf*.

Isak Dinesen: Pen name of a Danish author named Baroness Karen von Blixen-Finecke (1885–1962) who wrote *Out of Africa*.

Italo Calvino: An Italian writer (1923–1985).

Izaak Walton: An English writer (1593–1683), author of *The Compleat Angler*.

James Agee: An American novelist, screenwriter, journalist, poet, and film critic (1909–1955).

Jean Auel: An American writer (b. 1936), best known

for her "Earth's Children" books, set in prehistoric Europe, including *The Clan of the Cave Bear*.

Len Deighton: British author (b. 1929) of spy fiction and historical novels.

Leon Uris: American novelist (1924–2003) of historical fiction, including *Exodus* and *Trinity*.

Lew Wallace: An American lawyer, governor, Union general in the Civil War, but best remembered as the author of *Ben-Hur: A Tale of the Christ*.

Lin Yutang: A Chinese writer and inventor (1895–1976).

Mario Pei: An Italian-American linguist (1901–1978).

Ngaio Marsh: An author (of detective novels) and theater director from New Zealand (1895–1982).

Omar Khayyam: A Persian poet (1048–1131), best known for his collection of poetry, *The Rubaiyat of Omar Khayyam*.

Owen Wister: An American writer of western novels (1860–1938).

Saki: The pen name of the British writer H.H. Munro (1870–1916).

Sholem Asch: A Polish-born American writer (1880–1957).

Tama Janowitz: An American writer (b. 1957).

T.S. Eliot: An American poet, dramatist, and literary critic (1888–1965), best known for his works "The Love Song of J. Alfred Prufrock" and "The Waste Land." (His initials "TSE" often appear as an answer in crossword puzzles.)

Umberto Eco: An Italian writer (b. 1932), best known for his novels, *The Name of the Rose* and *Foucault's Pendulum*.

William Inge: An American playwright and novelist (1913–1973), best known for his scripts for *Picnic, Bus Stop, The Dark at the Top of the Stairs*, and *Splendor in the Grass*.

Aaron: The brother of Moses.

Abel: The son of Adam and Eve, killed by his brother
  Cain. (See: *Seth*)

Cain: The son of Adam and Eve, killed his brother *Abel*.
  (See: *Seth*)

Caleb: Best known as a spy.

Eli: Best known as Samuel's mentor.

Enos: A son of Seth.

Eremite: A hermit.

Esau: The son of Isaac and Rebekah and the older twin
  brother of Jacob, he was tricked by Jacob into giving
  up his birthright.

Essenes: A Jewish sect.

Ham: A son of Noah.

Lilith: Late medieval Jewish legend portrays her as the first wife of Adam.

Lot: A figure in the Bible whose wife was turned into a pillar of salt.

Seth: The son of Adam and Eve. (See: *Cain* and *Abel*)

Uriel: A Hebrew archangel.

Body Parts

Abs: Short for the "abdominal muscles." (See: *lats* and *pecs*)

Areola: The dark-colored skin around a nipple.

Cilia: The plural of "cilium," which is:
1. A short hair-like protrusion that one-celled organisms use to move;
2. An eyelash.

Femur: The thighbone. (See: *tarsus*, *tibia,* and *ulna*)

Gamete: A male or female cell that fuses with a gamete of the opposite sex to form a *zygote*.

Lats: Short for the "lateral muscles." (See: *abs, pecs* and *tarsus*)

Maw: The mouth, stomach, jaws, or gullet of a voracious animal, especially a carnivore.

Nape: The back of the neck. (See: *scruff*)

Pate: The crown of the head.

Pecs: Short for the "pectoral muscles." (See: *abs* and *lats*)

Plait: A braid (such as of hair or straw). (See: *tress*)

Rete: A network, especially of blood vessels or nerves.

Sac: A pouch or pouchlike structure in a plant or animal, sometimes filled with fluid.

Scruff: The back of the neck. (See: *nape*)

Snoot: A snout or nose. (Also: a snob)

Tarsus (singular)/Tarsi (plural): The ankle bones. (adjective: *tarsal*)

Tibia: The shin bone. (See: *femur, tarsus,* and *ulna*)

Tress:
1. a long lock of hair;
2. braid (See: *plait*)

Ulna: One of the bones (on the little finger side) of the forearm, next to the "radius." (See: *femur, tarsus,* and *tibia*)

Uvea: The pigmented middle layer of the eye.

Uvula: The fleshy lobe that hangs down at the back of the mouth.

Zygote: The cell formed by the union of two *gametes.*

Composers/Musicians

Al Hirt: A New Orleans trumpeter (1922–1999).

Amati family: A family of Italian violin makers (16th–17th centuries) in Cremona, Italy. Niccolo Amati (1596–1684) taught the famous violin makers Antonio Stradivari and Andrea Guarneri.

Brian Eno: An English musician (b. 1948).

Chick Corea: An American jazz pianist (b. 1941).

Dr. Dre: An American (hip hop) record producer, rapper, and actor (b. 1965).

Edouard Lalo: A French composer of Spanish descent (1823–1892).

Edward William Elgar: An English composer (1857–1934). Best know for his *Enigma Variations* and *Pomp and Circumstance.*

ELO: The Electric Light Orchestra, a rock music group.

Erik Satie: A French composer and pianist (1866–1925).

Esa-Pekka Salonen: A Finnish composer and conductor (b. 1958).

Franz Lehar: An Austrian composer of Hungarian descent (1870–1948), mainly known for his operettas (especially, *The Merry Widow*).

Giuseppe Verdi: An Italian composer (1813–1901) mainly of operas (including *Rigoletto, Il Travatore, La Traviata, Aida, Otello, and Falstaff*).

Janis Ian: An American songwriter, singer, and musician (b. 1951), best known for "Society's Child" (1966).

Lalo Schifrin: An Argentine pianist and composer (b. 1932), best known for the *Mission Impossible* theme.

Les Paul: An American jazz guitarist (b. 1915), a pioneer in the development of electric instruments.

Myra Hess: A British pianist (1890–1965).

Ned Rorem: An American composer (b. 1923).

Thomas Arne: An English composer (1710–1778), best known for the song, "Rule, Britannia!"

Uriah Heep: A British rock band since 1969. (Also see: *Uriah Heep*, under "Fictional Characters.")

Fictional Characters/ Literature/Titles

Abie: One of the characters in *Abie's Irish Rose*, a play in the 1920s.

Abou ben Adhem: The subject of a poem (First line: "Abou Ben Adhem [may his tribe increase]!") by James Henry Leigh Hunt.

Aida: The main character (an Ethiopian princess) of an opera of the same name by *Giuseppe Verdi*.

Alley Oop: A cartoon character (a prehistoric man). (His girlfriend's name was Oola.)

Apu: A character (an Indian immigrant and the proprietor of the Kwik-E-Mart) on *The Simpsons* TV series.

Ari Ben Canaan: The lead character in the novel, *Exodus* (by Leon Uris).

Ariel:
1. A character (a sprite serving the magician *Prospero*) in Shakespeare's play, *The Tempest*;
2. The main character ("Princess Ariel") in the Disney animated film, *The Little Mermaid* (1989).

Also:

3. An angel in Christianity and Judaism;
4. The first name of the American writer, Ariel Durant;
5. The first name of Ariel Sharon, Prime Minister of Israel (2001).

Ase: A character (a peasant's widow) in *Peer Gynt*, a play by Henrik Ibsen.

Asta: A character (played by a fox terrier) in the comedy detective film *The Thin Man*.

Auntie Em: Dorothy's aunt in *The Wizard of Oz*.

Ayla: A female character in Jean Auel's "Earth's Children" books.

Captain Nemo: The main character in Jules Verne's novels, *Twenty Thousand Leagues Under the Sea* (1870) and *The Mysterious Island* (1874).

Deanna Troi: The ship's counselor on *Star Trek: The Next Generation*.

Dora Copperfield: The first wife of the lead character in *David Copperfield* (by Charles Dickens).

Eeyore: A pessimistic, gloomy old donkey in the book series, *Winnie-the-Pooh* (by A. A. Milne).

Eloi: A spoiled, weak, post-human race in *The Time Machine* (1895) by H. G. Wells.

Elsie the Cow: The advertising mascot of the Borden Company.

Emma:
1. The title and the first name of the main character (Emma Woodhouse) of the comic novel (1816) by Jane Austen;
2. The first name of the main character in the novel, *Madame Bovary* (1856) by Gustave Flaubert.

Ena: Bambi's "aunt" in the 1942 Walt Disney animated feature, *Bambi*.

Enid: A character in the tales of *King Arthur and the Knights of the Round Table.* (Also: Enid, Oklahoma)

Ent: The Ents are a fictional race from Middle-earth, the fantasy world (in *The Hobbit* and *The Lord of the Rings*) created by J. R. R. Tolkien. (See: *Orc*)

Esme: A girl in a short story by J. D. Salinger.

Etta Kett: A character in a comic strip.

Faerie Queen, The: An epic poem by Edmund Spenser, first published in 1590.

Faust/Faustus: The protagonist of a popular German tale of a scholar who made a pact with the devil, used as the basis for many different fictional works.

Gil Blas: Title character of a novel by the French writer, Alain-Rene LeSage.

HAL: The "HAL 9000" talking and thinking computer in the 1968 Stanley Kubrick science fiction film, *2001: A Space Odyssey*.

Hud: A 1963 film with Paul Newman.

Ilsa: The character ("Ilsa Lund") played by Ingrid Bergman in the 1942 film *Casablanca*.

Jane Eyre: The main character and title of a novel by Charlotte Brontë.

Lara:
1. A character in the novel *Doctor Zhivago* by Boris Pasternak;

2. First name of the fictional heroine, Lara Croft;
3. Superman's biological mother.

Lili: The main character (played by Leslie Caron) of a musical movie (1953) of the same name.

Mortimer Snerd: The "dumb" dummy of ventriloquist Edgar Bergen (1903–1978).

Mr. Ed: The main character (a talking horse) and title of a TV situation comedy (1961–1966).

Nana: A dog, the pet of the Darling family in *Peter Pan*. (See: *Smee*)

Nell: The main character (played by Jodie Foster) and title of a 1994 movie.

Nora: The main character of *A Doll's House,* by Ibsen. Also:
1. The wife of James Joyce;
2. Nora Jones, an American pianist and singer-songwriter

Norma: The title of an opera by Vincenzo Bellini.

Odie: The lovable but dumb dog in the comic strip *Garfield* by Jim Davis.

Olan: A character in *The Good Earth*, by Pearl Buck.

Omoo: The title of a novel (the sequel to *Typee*) by Herman Melville.

Orc: Orcs are humanoid creatures from Middle-earth, the fantasy world (in *The Hobbit* and *The Lord of the Rings*) created by J. R. R. Tolkien. (See: *Ent*)

Pepe Le Moko: The title of a French film (1937).

Prince Igor: The title of an opera by Alexander Borodin.

Princess Leia: A character (played by Carrie Fisher) in the *Star Wars* story.

Prospero: The main character in Shakespeare's *The Tempest*. (See: *Ariel*)

Ren & Stimpy: Two cartoon characters (a Chihuahua and a cat).

Silas Marner: The title character in a novel (1861) by George Eliot (the pen name of Mary Ann Evans).

Smee: A pirate in the stage play and novel *Peter Pan* by J. M. Barrie. (See: *Nana*)

Swee' Pea: The baby adopted by Popeye.

Tige: The dog of Buster Brown (a comic strip character of the early 1900s).

Typee: The title (Full title: *Typee: A Peep at Polynesian Life*) of Herman Melville's first novel. (See: *Omoo*)

Ulee's Gold: A 1997 film starring Peter Fonda.

Uriah Heep : A character in the novel *David Copperfield* by Charles Dickens. (Also see *Uriah Heep* under "Composers/Musicians.")

Folklore, Gods, Myths, and the Supernatural

Adonis:
1. A youth loved by Aphrodite;
2. A very handsome young man

Aeneas: The hero of the *Aeneid*.

Aesir: The principal race of the Norse Gods.

Ananias:
1. An early Christian struck dead for lying;
2. A liar

Ariadne: A daughter of Minos who helped Theseus by giving him a magic sword and a ball of red fleece she was spinning so that he could find his way out of the Minotaur's labyrinth.

Astarte: The Phoenician goddess of fertility and sexual love.

Aten: In ancient Egyptian mythology, the creator of the universe, usually regarded as a sun god represented by the sun's disk.

Avatar:
1. The incarnation of a Hindu deity;
2. An incarnation in human form.

Baal: Any of numerous Canaanite and Phoenician local deities.

Charon: In Greek mythology, the man who ferries the dead across the river Styx.

Circe: A sorceress who changes Odysseus's men into swine.

Clio: The Greek muse of history.

Cronus: In Greek mythology, the leader and the youngest of the first generation of Titans, divine descendants of Gaia, the earth, and Uranus, the sky. He overthrew his father, Uranus, and ruled until he was overthrown by his own son, Zeus. (See: *Rhea*)

Dido: A legendary queen of Carthage (in Virgil's *Aeneid*).

Eos: The Greek goddess of dawn.

Erato: The Greek muse of lyric and love poetry.

Eris: The Greek goddess of discord.

Eros: The Greek god of love.

Faun: A woodland spirit in Roman mythology, similar to but gentler than the satyr. (See: *satyr*)

Gaea/Gaia: The Greek goddess personifying the Earth (Also: The idea that earth is a "living planet.")

Hecate: A Greek goddess associated with the underworld, night, sorcery, and witchcraft.

Ino: In Greek mythology, a mortal queen of Thebes.

Irene: The Greek goddess of peace.

Iris: The Greek goddess of the rainbow.

Ishtar: The goddess of fertility, love, spring, passion, sexuality, etc., in Assyrian and Babylonian mythology.

Isis: An Egyptian nature goddess and wife and sister of Osiris. (See: *Osiris*)

Lar (plural: Lares): A Roman god or spirit seen as guardian of the household.

Leda: In Greek mythology, the mother of Clytemnestra, Castor, Pollux, and Helen. (Zeus came and made love to her in the form of a swan.)

Ler/Lir: The Celtic/Irish god of the sea.

Loki: The Norse god of mischief.

Medea: In Greek mythology, the wife of Jason.

Morgan Le Fay: A powerful sorceress and antagonist of King Arthur and Guinevere.

Naiad: Water nymphs in Greek mythology.

Nereid: Sea nymphs in Greek mythology.

Nestor: A hero celebrated as an elderly and wise counselor (also noted for his bravery and speaking ability) to the Greeks at Troy.

Niobe: In Greek mythology, a mortal woman who turned to stone while weeping over the loss of her children.

Nymphs: In Greek mythology, female nature deities, represented as beautiful maidens.

Oberon: In medieval French and English folklore, the king of the fairies and husband of Titania.

Odin: The chief god in Norse mythology.

Ops: In Roman mythology, the goddess of abundance and fertility. (The wife of Saturn and the counterpart of Rhea in Greek mythology.)

Oracle: A priestess in ancient Greece through which a deity was believed to speak. (See: *seeress* and *sibyl*)

Oread: In Greek mythology, a mountain nymph.

Osiris: The Egyptian god of life, death, and fertility.

Peri: In Persian mythology, a beautiful and benevolent supernatural being or fairy.

Perseus: In Greek mythology, the slayer of Medusa.

Queen Mab: A fairy in English folklore.

Rhea: In Greek mythology, the sister and wife of Cronus and the mother of many of the other major gods. (See: *Cronus*)

Roc: A legendary bird of great size.

Satyr: A sylvan deity in Greek mythology with the form of a young human but having characteristics of a horse or goat, living in the woods or forest and fond of revelry.

Seeress: A woman who has the gift of prophecy. (See: *oracle* and *sibyl*)

Shiva: The Hindu god of destruction and regeneration.

Sibyl: A prophetess. (See: *oracle* and *seeress*)

Sylph: An imaginary or mythological spirit with the form of a slender, graceful girl or woman.

Thalia: The Greek muse of comedy.

Theseus: A legendary king of Athens who, with the help of *Ariadne*, slew the Minotaur.

Wraith: A ghost or specter.

Yeti: The Abominable Snowman.

Generic Roles/Occupations

Ace:
1. A person who excels at something;
2. The best pitcher on a baseball team;
3. A combat pilot who has brought down at least five enemy planes. (See: *maven* and *oner*.) (Also appears in crossword puzzles as "acer," i.e., one who "aces.")

Alum(nus) : Someone who has attended or graduated from a particular school, college, or university. (Also: Alumna, Alumnae, Alumni)

Amah : A female servant in Eastern Asia; especially: a Chinese nurse.

Ami(e): The French word for "friend."

Angel: The backer of a theatrical production.

Arbitrageur: A kind of financial trader. (Often abbreviated in crossword puzzles as "arb.")

Augur: One who can foretell future events by omens.

Bos'n: The short form for "boatswain," a petty officer on a merchant ship or a naval warrant officer.

Capo: The head of a branch of an organized crime syndicate.

Cat's Paw: One used by another as a tool; a dupe.

Doge: Starting in the eighth century, A.D., the chief magistrate in the Republic of Venice (Italy).

Doña: Used as a title (in Portuguese or Spanish) prefixed to a woman's Christian name.

Esne:

1. A member of the lowest feudal class, attached to the land owned by a lord and required to perform labor in return for certain legal or customary rights;
2. An agricultural laborer under various similar systems, especially in 18th- and 19th-century Russia and eastern Europe. (See: *helot, liege, serf, thane,* and *vassal.*)

Fabulist:

1. A creator or writer of fables;
2. A liar.

Fop:

1. A foolish or silly person;
2. A man who is devoted to or vain about his appearance or dress.

Gob: A sailor. (See: *salt, swab, tar*)

Helot: A serf or slave. (See: *esne, liege, serf, thane,* and *vassal*)

Jingo: One characterized by "jingoism," i.e., extreme chauvinism or nationalism marked especially by a belligerent foreign policy.

Laird: A Scottish term for a landed proprietor.

Legate: A (usually official) emissary.

Liege:
1. A vassal bound to feudal service and allegiance;
2. A feudal superior to whom allegiance and service are due. (See: *esne, helot, serf, thane,* and *vassal*)

Maven: A Yiddish word for one who is experienced or knowledgeable; an expert. (See: *ace* and *oner*)

Mensch: A Yiddish word for a person of integrity and honor. (See: *virago*)

Naif: A naïve person.

Oda(lisque):
1. A female slave;
2. A concubine in a harem.

Oner: A unique or extraordinary person or thing. (See: *ace* and *maven*)

Ostler: One who takes care of horses or mules. (A variation of the word, "hostler.")

Parvenu(e): One who has recently or suddenly risen to an unaccustomed position of wealth or power but has not yet gained the prestige, dignity, or manner associated with it.

Pleb(eian): One of the common people (especially in ancient Rome).

Plebe: A freshman at a military or naval academy.

Poseur:
1. A person who pretends to be what he or she is not;
2. An affected or insincere person.

Prole(tarian): A member of the lower or laboring class.

Rake: A dissolute person; libertine. (See: *roué*)

Rasta(farian): An adherent of Rastafarianism (a religious movement among black Jamaicans).

Reeve:
1. In some parts of Canada, the elected president of a town council;
2. Any of various minor officers of parishes or other local authorities;
3. A bailiff or steward of a manor in the later medieval period;
4. A high officer of local administration appointed by the Anglo-Saxon kings.

Roué: A man devoted to a life of sensual pleasure. (See: *rake*)

Sainte: The French word for "saint" (often used in crosswords in its abbreviated form, "Ste.")

Salt: A sailor. (See: *gob, swab, tar*)

Scion:

1. A descendent, child, especially: a descendent of a wealthy, aristocratic, or influential family; an heir. (See: *sire*)

Also

2. A detached living portion of a plant (such as a bud or shoot) joined to a stock in grafting.

Serf: A member of a servile feudal class bound to the land and subject to the will of its owner. (See: *esne, helot, liege,* and *vassal*)

Sire:

1. A father;
2. The male parent of an animal, especially of a domestic animal. (See: *scion*)

Sniggler: One who "sniggles," i.e., fishes for eels.

Steno (grapher):

1. A writer of shorthand;
2. A person employed chiefly to take and transcribe dictation. (Often used in crossword puzzles in conjunction with a clue that makes a pun on the expression, "steno pool.")

Stentor: A person who has a loud voice. (Named for Stentor, a Greek herald in the Trojan War noted for his loud voice.)

Swab: A sailor. (See: *salt, swab, tar*)

Swain: A male admirer or suitor. (See: *esne, helot, liege, serf,* and *vassal*)

Tar: A sailor. (See: *gob, salt, swab*)

Tec: Short for "detective."

Thane: A Scottish feudal lord.

Tyro: A beginner, novice, amateur. (Compare: *ace* and *maven*)

Vassal: A feudal tenant. (See: *esne, helot, liege, serf,* and *thane*)

Virago:

1. A loud, overbearing woman;
2. A woman of great stature, strength, and courage. (See: *mensch*)

Yegg: A slang word for a safecracker.

Groups

Ainu: An indigenous people of the northern Japanese islands (or a member of that group).

Aleut: A member of a people of the Aleutian Islands and the western part of the Alaska Peninsula.

Boer: A South African of Dutch or Huguenot descent.

BPOE: Stands for the "Benevolent and Protective Order of Elks" (or, colloquially, the "best people on earth.")

Carib: A member of a group of Indian people of the Caribbean.

Celt: A Gael, Highland Scot, Irishman, Welshman, Cornishman, or Breton.

Coterie: An intimate and often exclusive group with a unifying common interest or purpose.

Cree: An American Indian people of eastern Canada.

Eli: A student at Yale University.

Esth.: Abbreviation for an Estonian.

Gael: A Celtic, especially Gaelic-speaking, inhabitant of Ireland, Scotland, or the Isle of Man.

Inca(n): A member of the Quechuan peoples of Peru who were conquered by the Spanish under Pizarro.

Lett: A Latvian.

Mede: A native or inhabitant of ancient Media (in Persia).

Nez Perce: An Indian tribe of the Pacific Northwest.

Oto(e): An Indian tribe of the Midwest.

Pict: A member of an ancient group of people of the north of Scotland.

Pima: A member of an Indian tribe of southern Arizona and northern Mexico.

SDS: The abbreviated name of the "Students for a Democratic Society," a radical activist group of the 1960s.

Sinn Fein: A nationalist Irish group or political party.

SLA: The abbreviated name of the so-called "Symbionese Liberation Army," a small, violent, and radical paramilitary group of the mid-1970s in California.

Tamil: An ethnic group on the Indian subcontinent, especially in Southern India and Sri Lanka.

UCLAn: A student at UCLA (the University of California at Los Angeles).

Ute: A member of an American Indian people originally ranging through Utah, Colorado, Arizona, and New Mexico.

Abel Tasman: A Dutch explorer (1603–1659).

Aristotle ("Ari") Onassis: Greek shipping magnate (1906–1975), married Jacqueline Kennedy.

Catherine Parr: The last wife of King Henry VIII of England (1512–1548).

Elihu Root: American lawyer and statesman (1845–1937) and recipient of the Nobel Peace Prize in 1912.

Ernesto "Che" Guevara: An Argentine-born Marxist revolutionary (1928–1967) who joined Fidel Castro's revolutionary movement, which seized power in Cuba in 1959. He was executed in Bolivia in 1967.

Este: A European noble family for a thousand years (from the tenth century A.D.), identified with the city of Ferrara.

General Tso: A Chinese military leader (1812–1885) (best known as the namesake for the popular dish, "General Tso's chicken").

65

Horace Mann: An American education reformer and abolitionist (1796–1859).

Jacob Riis: A Danish-American muckraking journalist and social reformer (1849–1914).

Jane Addams: An American social worker, sociologist, philosopher, and reformer (1860–1935), cofounder of Hull House in Chicago, and the first American woman to win the Nobel Peace Prize.

Jeanne D'Arc (Joan of Arc): A French national heroine and Roman Catholic saint (1412–1431).

Judge Lance Ito: The presiding judge (b. 1952) in the O. J. Simpson trial.

Lao-Tse/Lao-Tsu: An ancient Chinese philosopher.

Leopold and Loeb: Defendants in a notorious Chicago trial for the 1924 murder of a teenager.

Marquis de Sade: A French aristocrat and writer (1740–1814) of violent pornography.

Marshal Ferdinand Foch: A general (1851–1929) in

the French army and the supreme commander of the allied armies during World War I.

Marshal Michel Ney: A French military commander (1769–1815) during the French Revolution and the Napoleonic wars.

Mary Baker Eddy: Founder (1821–1910) of the "Church of Christ, Scientist" (better known as the "Christian Science Church").

Nellie Bly: An American journalist (1864–1922) who wrote about social issues.

Nikola Tesla: A Serbian-American electrical engineer and inventor (1856–1943), inventor of the"Tesla coil."

Oona Chaplin: The daughter of playwright Eugene O'Neill and the fourth wife of actor Charlie Chaplin (1926–1991).

Queen Noor: The fourth wife and widow (b. 1951) of the late King Hussein of Jordan.

Rene Coty: The president of France (1882–1962) from 1954 to 1959.

Saint Elmo: The patron saint of sailors.

Seth Thomas: An American clock maker (1785–1859).

Silas Deane: A delegate to the American Continental Congress (1737–1789) and later the United States' first foreign diplomat.

Toots Shor: During the 1940s and 1950s, the proprietor of a legendary restaurant (Toots Shor's) in Manhattan (1903–1977).

Venerable Bede: An English monk (672–735), best known as the author of *The Ecclesiastical History of the English People.*

Wyatt Earp: A saloon keeper and law officer (1848–1929) in the Old West, best known for his participation in the gunfight at the O.K. Corral (1881, in Tombstone, Arizona).

Legal People

Alienee: One to whom property is transferred.

Amicus Curiae: The Latin term for a "friend of the

court," i.e., one who is not a party to a litigation but who is permitted by the court to advise it.

Living Things (and Their Parts)

Abele: A name for the white poplar (tree).

Acer: A maple tree.

Agave: A succulent plant of the southern and western United States and in South America.

Aloe: A succulent plant (often mentioned in crossword puzzles in connection with aloe vera, an aloe whose extract is used in cosmetics and skin creams).

Anise: A Eurasian herb of the carrot family that yields aromatic seeds (aniseed).

Anther: The part of a flower that produces pollen. (See: *pistil, sepal,* and *stamen*)

Areca: A tropical Old World palm. (See: *nipa, raffia,* and *sago*)

Aril: The exterior of some seeds.

Arista: A bristlelike structure or appendage.

Arum: An Old World plant with arrowhead-shaped leaves.

Aster: A fall-blooming herb, also called a "Michaelmas Daisy."

Awn: A slender hair- or bristle-like appendage on some cereals or grasses.

Axil: The angle between a branch or leaf and the axis from which it arises.

Coir: The fiber obtained from the husk of a coconut, used chiefly in making rope and matting.

Copse: A thicket of small trees or shrubs; a grove.

Ergot: A fungus that grows on the seed of a cereal or grass.

Ilex: Any of various trees or shrubs of the genus *Ilex* (holly).

Liana: A woody vine of tropical rain forests.

Nipa : A Southeast Asian palm. (See: *areca, raffia,* and *sago*)

Oca/Oka: A South American wood sorrel (or its edible tuber).

Orris root: The fragrant root of some species of iris, used in perfumes.

Osier:
1. A kind of willow or dogwood;
2. A willow rod used in basketry.

Papaw/Pawpaw:
1. Papaya;
2. A North American tree of the custard-apple family (or its large edible fruit).

Pistil: A single "carpel" (a female reproductive organ of a flower). (See: *anther, sepal,* and *stamen*)

Posy/Posey: A small bouquet or bunch of flowers.

Raffia: A large palm (or its fiber, which is used as cord for tying and weaving). (See: *areca, nipa,* and *sago*)

Sago: A kind of palm (or its starch, which is used in foods and as textile stiffening). (See: *areca, nipa,* and *raffia*)

Sedge: A kind of marsh plant that is similar to a grass or rush.

Sego: A lily that is the state flower of Utah.

Sepal: An individual unit of the calyx of a flower. (See: *anther, pistil,* and *stamen*)

Seta (Plural: Setae): A stiff hair, bristle, or bristlelike process or part on an organism.

Sisal: A Mexican and Central American agave plant widely cultivated for its large, sword-shaped leaves that yield stiff fibers used for cordage and rope.

Stamen: The pollen-producing male organ of a flower. (See: *anther, pistil,* and *sepal*)

Stele: The central portion of a vascular plant.

Stoma: A small opening in a plant or animal.

Yew: A poisonous evergreen tree or shrub (or its wood).

Middle Easterners

Aga/Agha: A civil or military leader, especially in Turkey.

Amir/Ameer/ Emeer/Emir: A prince, chieftain, or governor, especially in the Middle East.

Bey: An Ottoman ruler.

Pasha: A military or civil officer, especially in Turkey and northern Africa.

Sabra: A native-born Israeli.

Satrap:
1. The governor of a province in ancient Persia;
2. A ruler;
3. A subordinate bureaucrat or official.

Military People

Aide-de-camp: A military officer acting as secretary and confidential assistant to a superior officer of general or flag rank.

NCO: Abbreviation for a "non-commissioned officer."

Poilu: A French soldier, especially in World War I.

Politicians/Statesmen

Abba Eban: An Israeli diplomat (1915–2002).

Adlai E. Stevenson: An Illinois governor (1900–1965), unsuccessful presidential contender in 1952 and 1956, and later U.S. Ambassador to the U.N. (His initials "AES" appear in crossword puzzles more often than his name.)

Czar/Tsar: A Slavonic term for certain monarchs, especially in imperial Russia.

Desmond Tutu: A South African cleric, activist (b. 1931) and recipient of the Nobel Peace Prize (in 1984).

Diet: Japan's legislature.

Duma: A representative assembly in Russia.

Dwight David Eisenhower: The Supreme Commander

of the Allied Forces in World War II (1890–1969) and the thirty-fourth president of the United States (1953–1961). (His initials "DDE" appear in puzzles more often than his name.) (See: *Mamie Eisenhower*)

Ehud Barak: An Israeli politician (b. 1942).

Idi Amin: The former president/dictator of Uganda (1924–2003).

Imre Nagy: A Hungarian politician and Prime Minister (1896–1958).

Josip Broz Tito: The leader of Yugoslavia (b. 1892) from World War II until his death in 1980.

Konrad Adenauer: A German political leader (1876–1967) (often referred to in crossword puzzles by his nickname, "Der Alte [The Old Man]").

Mamie Eisenhower: The wife of Dwight David Eisenhower.

Mobuto Sese Seko: The former president of Zaire (now the Democratic Republic of the Congo) (1930–1997).

Solon:

1. A wise and skillful lawgiver;
2. A member of a legislative body.

Syngman Rhee: The first president of South Korea (1875–1965).

Religious People

Abbé: A French abbot.

B'nai Brith: A Jewish service organization.

Imam: A Moslem religious leader.

Scientists

André-Marie Ampère: A French physicist (1775–1836).

Asa Grey: An American botanist (1810–1888).

Singers

ABBA: A Swedish pop music group from 1972 until 1982. (The musical, "Mamma Mia!," is based on their songs.)

Abbe Lane: An American singer and actress (b. 1932).

Anita Baker: An African-American rhythm-and-blues singer-songwriter (b. 1958).

Anita Bryant: An American singer (b. 1940).

Arlo Guthrie: An American folk singer (b. 1947), best known for his song, "Alice's Restaurant," and as the son of Woody Guthrie.

Edie Adams: An American singer (b. 1927), married to Ernie Kovacs until his death in 1962.

Edith Piaf: A French singer (1915–1963), best known for her song, "La Vie en Rose."

Etta James: An American blues, R & B, and gospel singer (b. 1938).

Frankie Laine: An American singer (1913–2007), best known for his songs, "Mule Train" and "Riders in the Sky."

India Arie: An American soul and R & B singer-songwriter (b. 1975).

Jenny Lind: A Swedish-born singer (1820–1887), known as the "Swedish Nightingale."

Kiri Te Kanawa: A New Zealand–born opera singer (b. 1944).

Lena Horne: An African-American singer and actress (b. 1917), best known for her version of "Stormy Weather."

Lotte Lenya: An Austrian-born singer and actress (1898–1981), best known for her performance in *The Threepenny Opera*.

Paul Anka: A Lebanese-Canadian singer, songwriter, and actor (b. 1941), best known for his song "Diana," and for writing "She's a Lady," "My Way," and the *The Tonight Show* theme.

Sade Adu: An Afro-European singer, composer, song-writer, and record producer (b. 1959).

Toni Tennille: Born in 1940, she was one-half of the 1970s singing duo, "Captain and Tennille."

Yma Sumac: A Peruvian singer (b. 1922).

PART TWO

PLACES

Biblical/Fictional/Imaginary Places

Edom: A land in the Bible.

Endor:
1. A village in the Bible (where the "Witch of Endor" lived);
2. In the film *Return of the Jedi*, Endor is a planet orbited by the forest moon of Endor;
3. In J. R. R. Tolkien's fictional world of Arda, Endor is the Quenya name for the continent of Middle-earth.

Lethe: In Greek mythology, a river in Hades. (See: *Styx*)

Nod: The Biblical land to which Cain was banished.

Styx: In Greek mythology, the principal river of the Underworld. (See: *Lethe*)

Tara (plantation):
1. The home of the kings of Ireland;
2. The name of the plantation which is the home of Scarlett O'Hara in *Gone with the Wind*.

Bodies of Water

Aden, Gulf of: An arm of the Indian Ocean between Aden and Somalia.

Aral Sea: A lake in Asia between Kazakhstan and Kyrgyzstan.

Azov, Sea of: A gulf of the Black Sea.

Buildings/Rooms/Parts of Buildings and Rooms

Abattoir: A slaughterhouse.

Anta: A pilaster forming the end of a projecting lateral wall and constituting one boundary of the portico.

Apiary: A place where bees are kept.

Apse: A projecting part of a building, such as a church. (See: *nave*)

Atelier: An artist's or designer's studio or workroom; workshop.

Atrium (Plural: Atria):
1. A rectangular open patio;
2. A many-storied court or hall (as in a hotel), usually with a skylight, into which rooms open at one or more levels.

Auberge: An inn.

Bodega:
1. A small grocery store, sometimes combined with a wine shop, in certain Hispanic communities;
2. A warehouse for the storage of wine.

Cote: A small shed or shelter for sheep or birds.

Dacha: A Russian country cottage.

Dado:
1. The section of a pedestal above the base;
2. The lower portion of the wall of a room, decorated differently from the upper section, as with panels.

Ell: An extension at a right angle to a building.

Gaol: The British spelling of "jail."

Hogan: A Navaho Indian dwelling.

Imaret: A Turkish inn.

Ingle: A fireplace.

Kirk: A Scottish church.

Lanai: A Hawaiian porch or veranda.

Loo: A British term for a toilet.

Manse:
1. A minister's dwelling;
2. A large impressive residence.

Nave: The long central hall in a church. (See: *apse*)

Newel:
1. A vertical post or support at the center of a circular staircase;
2. A post that supports a handrail at the bottom or at the landing of a staircase.

Oriel: A large bay window.

Sconce: A decorative wall bracket for holding candles or light.

Seraglio:

1. A harem;
2. A palace of a sultan.

Serai:

1. A hotel, inn;
2. A palace of a sultan.

Soffit: The underside of a part of a building (such as an arch, an overhang, or a staircase).

Stoa: An ancient Greek portico, covered walk, or colonnade.

Cities/Towns

Accra: The capital of Ghana.

Agana: The capital of Guam.

Ascot: A village southwest of London (associated with the Ascot Racecourse).

Assisi: A town in central Italy (associated with St. Francis).

Asti: A wine-growing town/region of Italy.

Dieppe: A city and port in northern France, the scene of fighting in World War II.

Doha: The capital city/port of Qatar.

Ede: A town in the Netherlands.

Edina: A suburb of Minneapolis, Minnesota.

Enid: A city in Oklahoma.

Enna: A city in Sicily (not to be confused with *Etna*, the volcano).

Essen: A city on the Ruhr River in Germany.

Etah: A town in India.

Moab:
1. A city in Utah;
2. In Biblical times, a kingdom east of the Dead Sea.

Muscat: The capital of Oman.

Ocala: A city in Florida, near Gainesville.

Odense: A city in Denmark.

Odessa:
1. A city in Texas;
2. A city in the Ukraine (site of a workers' uprising by the crew of the battleship *Potemkin* in 1905).

Oran: A city and port in Algeria.

Orem: A city in Utah.

Orono: A town in Maine.

Ostia: A town in central Italy at the mouth of the Tiber River (and near the site of an ancient town of the same name that served as a port for Rome).

Otaru: City and port on the island of Hokkaido (Japan).

Sana(a): The capital of Yemen.

Sault Sainte Marie: A city in Ontario, Canada (near the Soo Canals).

St.-Lo: A town in Normandy, France.

Tirana: The capital and largest city of Albania.

Truro:
1. A town in southwest England;
2. A town near the tip of Cape Cod, Massachusetts.

Ulan Bator: The capital of Mongolia.

Counties/Countries/Nations/States

Assam: A state in northeast India near the Himalayas.

Bama: Short for "Alabama."

Eire: The Irish name for "Ireland" in English. (See: *Erin*)

Erin: A romantic/poetic name for Ireland. (See: *Eire*)

Norge: The Norwegian name for Norway.

Oman: A sultanate on the southeast coast of the Arabian Peninsula.

Otero: A county in New Mexico.

U.A.E.: The United Arab Emirates.

Ulster: Northern Ireland.

Uri: A canton in Switzerland (often mentioned in cross-words in association with William Tell).

Generic Geographic Places

Abyss: An immeasurably deep gulf or pit.

Adit: An almost horizontal entrance to a mine.

Aerie: A bird's nest on a cliff or mountaintop.

Arete: A sharp-crested mountain ridge.

Brae: A Scottish word for a hillside, especially along a river.

Cru: A vineyard or wine-producing region in France.

Dale: A valley.

Esker: A long, narrow, winding ridge of sand, gravel, and boulders left by streams which flowed within and under glaciers in regions of Europe and North America.

Fen: A kind of wetland that has characteristic flora (such as reeds and sedges).

Fief(dom) : A feudal estate.

Floe: A large sheet of ice floating on a body of water.

Lea: A grassland, pasture.

Littoral: A coastal region, or the banks of a river, lake, or estuary. (The "littoral zone" is the area between high and low tides.)

Ria: A coastal area that has become submerged; an estuary.

Rill: A very small brook. (Also: A long, narrow valley on the moon's surface.)

Shoal:
1. A shallow place in a body of water;
2. A sandbank/bar that makes the water above it shallow.

Swale: A low-lying, often wet, stretch of land.

Tarn: A small, steep-banked mountain lake or pool.

Tor: A high, craggy hill.

Vale: A wide river valley.

Wadi: An Arabic word for a valley or dry riverbed.

Weir:
1. A fence in water to catch fish;
2. A dam in a stream or river to raise the water level or to divert its flow (often into a mill pond).

Historical Places/Landmarks

Agora: In ancient Greece, a marketplace.

Agra: The site of the Taj Mahal in India.

Appian Way: The most important ancient Roman road.

Arthur Ashe Stadium: The main tennis stadium of the U.S. Open, located in Flushing Meadows Park in northern Queens, New York City. (See: *Shea Stadium*)

Aswan: A city in southern Egypt near where two dams (the newer Aswan High Dam and the older Aswan Dam) stretch across the Nile.

Cairn: A mound of stones erected as a memorial or marker. (See: *stela*)

Edo: The former name of Tokyo.

Estes Park: A town in Colorado.

Eton: A town in Berkshire, England, across the Thames from Windsor, and the site of the famous "public" school, Eton College.

La Scala: A famous opera house in Milan, Italy.

Shea Stadium: A baseball stadium in Flushing, New York, home to the New York Mets. (See: *Arthur Ashe Stadium*)

Sidon: An ancient Phoenician city on the coast of the Mediterranean in what is now Lebanon. (See: *Tyre*)

Soo Canal: Water "locks" that allow ships to travel between Lake Superior and the lower Great Lakes.

SSR: An abbreviation for "Soviet Socialist Republic," a member nation of the former Soviet Union.

Stela: An upright stone or slab with an inscribed or

sculptured surface, used as a monument or as a commemorative tablet in the face of a building. (See: *cairn*)

Trevi Fountain: A famous fountain in Rome.

Tyre: An ancient Phoenician city on the coast of the Mediterranean in what is now Lebanon. (See: *Sidon*)

UAR: An abbreviation for the "United Arab Republic," a nation that was formed by the union of Egypt and Syria (1958–61).

Islands

Ait: A little island.

Atoll: A ringlike coral island and reef around a lagoon.

Attu: An island in the Aleutian Islands of Alaska.

Cay: A small, low island composed largely of coral or sand.

Cebu: An island of the central Philippines.

Elba: An island in the Mediterranean between Corsica and the mainland where Napoleon was exiled after his abdication in 1814 (not to be confused with *Elbe*, the river).

Iona: A small island in the Inner Hebrides in Scotland.

Isle(t): A little island (in French: *ile*) (in Spanish: *isla*)

Isle of Wight: An island off the southern English coast.

Lido: An island reef of northeast Italy separating the lagoon of Venice from the Adriatic Sea.

Prince Edward Island: A Canadian island and province of the same name. (Its abbreviation "PEI" appears in crossword puzzles more often than its full name does.)

Upolu: An island in Samoa.

Mountains/Volcanoes

Alai: A mountain range in southwest Kyrgyzstan.

Eiger: A mountain in central Switzerland.

Etna, Mount: A volcano in Italy, northeast of Sicily (not to be confused with *Enna*, the city).

Ossa, Mount: A mountain (mentioned in Greek mythology) in Greece.

Uinta Mountains: Mountains in Utah.

Ural Mountains: Mountains in Russia and Kazakhstan, usually considered to be the dividing line between Europe and Asia.

Outer Space

Ara: A constellation in the southern sky.

Ariel: A moon of the planet Uranus (named for a character in *The Tempest,* by Shakespeare).

Deneb: The brightest star in the constellation Cygnus.

Rill: A long narrow valley on the moon's surface. (Also: A very small brook.)

Rivers

Aar(e): A river in Switzerland.

Amur: A river that forms the border between the Russian Far East and Manchuria in China.

Arno: A river that flows through Florence.

Cam: A river in England that flows through Cambridge.

Dee: There are several rivers named "Dee" in Scotland, Great Britain, and Ireland.

Ebro: A river in northeast Spain.

Eddy: A current, as of water or air, moving contrary to the direction of the main current, especially in a circular motion.

Elbe: A river that flows through the Czech Republic and Germany into the North Sea (not to be confused with *Elba*, the island).

Isere: A river that flows from the Alps in France into the Rhone.

Lena: A river in Siberia.

Meuse: A river that flows through France and Belgium into the North Sea.

Neva: A Russian river that flows to the Gulf of Finland at St. Petersburg.

Oder: A river that flows from the Czech Republic and forms part of the border between Poland and Germany, finally flowing into the Baltic Sea.

Oise: A river of northern France that flows into the *Seine*.

Orinoco: A Venezuelan river that flows to the Atlantic Ocean.

Ouse: There are two rivers in England by this name.

Ruhr: A river in Germany that flows to the Rhine. (Also refers to the industrial district in the valley of the Ruhr.)

Saar: A river that flows from France to Germany.

Saone: A river in France flowing into the Rhone.

Seine: The river that flows through Paris.

Tagus: A river that flows west from Spain through Portugal to the Atlantic.

Thames: The river that flows through London.

Uele: A river in central Africa.

Yalu: A river that runs along the border between China and North Korea.

Yser: A river of Belgium and France that flows into the North Sea.

PART THREE

THINGS

ABO: The "A-B-O" blood-typing system.

AEC : The "Atomic Energy Commission," was established after World War II. It was replaced by the *NRC*.

AEF: The "Allied Expeditionary Force" in World War I.

AKA: "Also known as."

APO: "Army Post Office."

ASCAP: "The American Society of Composers, Authors, and Publishers."

BBL: Abbreviation for one "barrel" of oil or natural gas.

BMI: The "British Music Society," an organization that protects music composers' rights (not to be confused with *EMI*).

D'oh: Homer Simpson's catchphrase in the long-running animated series *The Simpsons*.

DSC: The "Distinguished Service Cross," an Australian, British (naval), and American military award.

DSO: The "Distinguished Service Order," a British military decoration.

EEE: A large shoe width.

EMI: A major British music label (not to be confused with *BMI*).

EMT: An "Emergency Medical Technician."

ERA: "Earned Run Average" (in baseball).

Esc: The "escape" key on a computer keyboard.

EST: The "Erhard Seminars Training," a 1970s "new-age" group-awareness training.

ETA: "Estimated Time of Arrival." (See: *ETD*)

ETD: "Estimated Time of Departure." (See: *ETA*)

ETO: The "European Theater of Operations," used in the U.S. during World War II to refer to U.S. military operations in Europe.

Ezine/E-zine: A periodic publication distributed by e-mail or posted on a website. (See: *Zine*).

GED: The "General Educational Development Test" (which certifies that the taker has attained high school–level academic skills).

GTO: "Gran Turismo Omologato," a model name used on several cars (and the name of a popular 1964 song).

HRE: The "Holy Roman Empire" (843–1806).

ILA: The "International Longshoreman's Association."

ILO: The "International Labor Organization," an agency of the United Nations.

INRI: An abbreviation of the Latin phrase, "Iesvs Nazarenvs Rex Ivdaeorvm," ("Jesus the Nazarene, the King of the Jews.")

ITT: "ITT Corporation" is a large American manufacturing company that is a successor to a large conglomerate, originally called "International Telephone and Telegraph," which owned a variety of businesses during the 1960s.

LEM: The "Lunar Excursion Module," the lander portion of the spacecraft used during the Apollo missions to the moon.

LIRR: The "Long Island Rail Road," a commuter line in New York.

LST: A so-called "Landing Ship (for) Tanks," an amphibious craft developed by the Allies during World War II to support amphibious operations.

MBE: "Member [of the] British Empire," a British honorary title. (See: *OBE*)

Mdse: Abbreviation for "merchandise."

NEA: "National Education Association," a teachers' union.

NRA:
1. The "National Rifle Association";
2. The "National Recovery Administration," a part of FDR's New Deal program. (See: *WPA*)

NRC: The "Nuclear Regulatory Commission," which in 1975 took over the role of oversight of nuclear energy matters and nuclear safety from the *AEC*.

OBE: "Officer [of the] British Empire," a British honorary title. (See: *MBE*)

OCS: "Officer Candidate School."

OED: The *Oxford English Dictionary.*

OSS: The "Office of Strategic Services," an American intelligence agency that was formed during World War II and that was the precursor of the present-day CIA.

OTB: "Off-Track Betting."

OTC: "Over-the-counter" (medications).

QED: Abbreviation of the Latin phrase, *"quod erat demonstrandum"* (literally, "which was to be demonstrated"). Used to indicate that something (such as a mathematical statement) has been definitively proven.

REM: "Rapid eye movements," the rapid, periodic, jerky movement of the eyes during certain stages of the sleep cycle when dreaming takes place.

Ret: "Retired."

RICO: The "Racketeer Influenced and Corrupt Organizations" Act, a federal law that provides for extended penalties for criminal acts performed as part of an ongoing criminal organization.

RPI: "Rensselaer Polytechnic Institute," a technological university in Troy, New York.

Rte: Route.

RUR: Short for *Rossum's Universal Robots,* a science-fiction play by Karel Capek.

SASE: "Self-addressed stamped envelope."

SLR: A "Single-Lens Reflex" camera.

SPF: "Sun Protection Factor," a measure of the effectiveness of a sunscreen.

SQMI: An abbreviation for *"Senatus Populusque Romanus"*("The Senate and People of Rome").

SRO:
1. "Standing Room Only";
2. "Single Room Occupancy" (hotel).

SSN: "Social Security Number."

SSS: "Selective Service System."

SST: "Super-Sonic Transport" (often used in crosswords in relation to the Concorde supersonic airplane).

Sta: Station.

Stat: Statistic.

STP: Originally stood for, "Scientifically Treated Petroleum," but now STP is a trade name for an automotive oil and fuel additive company.

TBA: "To Be Announced."

TID: "*Ter In Die*," Latin abbreviation for "three times a day" (used in medical prescriptions).

TLC: "Tender Loving Care."

UTEP: The "University of Texas [at] El Paso."

WPA: The "Works Progress Administration" (later, "Works Projects Administration"), a U.S. government employment agency (1935–1943). (See: *NRA*)

YTD: "Year to Date."

Zine : Short for "Fanzine": A small circulation, noncom-
mercial or self-published publication of minority interest or unconventional subject matter. (See: *e-zine*)

Abstract Ideas/Nouns

Ambit:
1. The bounds or limits of a place;
2. A sphere of action; scope.

Ana: A literary collection (of sayings, anecdotes, etc.).

Aura:
1. A distinctive atmosphere/energy surrounding or
emanating from something or a living being;
2. A luminous radiation. (See: *aureole* and *nimbus*)

Aureole:
1. A radiant light around a representation of a sacred
being; halo; *aura*;
2. The luminous area around a bright light. (See: *nimbus*)

Brio: Vivacity, verve.

Canard: A false or unfounded report or story; a groundless rumor or belief.

Chit: A statement of an amount owed for food and drink.

Elan: Vigorous spirit or enthusiasm.

Epitaph:
1. An inscription on or at a tomb or a grave in memory of the one buried there;
2. A brief statement commemorating a deceased person or something past.

Ethos: The distinguishing sentiment, moral nature, or guiding beliefs of a person, group, or institution.

Facet:
1. A small plane or surface, as on a cut gem;
2. One of numerous aspects, as of a subject.

Heft: Weight; heaviness; bulk.

Ilk: Sort, kind.

Mien: Bearing, demeanor, appearance, aspect.

Moue: A little grimace; pout.

Nimbus:

1. A cloudy radiance said to surround a classical deity when on earth;
2. A radiant light that appears usually in the form of a circle or halo about or over the head in the representation of a god, demigod, saint, or sacred person such as a king or an emperor;
3. A splendid atmosphere or aura, as of glamour, that surrounds a person or thing;
4. A rain cloud, especially a low, dark layer of clouds such as a nimbostratus.

Oater: A novel, story, motion picture, or broadcast dealing with life in the western U.S., especially in the latter half of the nineteenth century.

Obeah:

1. A form of religious belief of African origin, practiced in some parts of the West Indies, involving sorcery;
2. An object, charm, or fetish used in the practice of this religion.

Odium:

1. The state or quality of being subjected to hatred or contempt resulting from despicable, hateful, or detestable conduct or blameworthy circumstances;

2. Strong dislike, contempt, hatred, or aversion;
3. A state of disgrace, disrepute, or infamy.

Olio : A mixture or medley; a hodgepodge.

Onus:
1. Obligation;
2. Blame.

Orb:
1. A spherical body, especially a spherical celestial object;
2. Eye.

Orison: Prayer.

Pavane:
1. A slow, stately court dance of the 16th and 17th centuries;
2. A piece of music for this dance.

Plat:
1. A small piece of ground; plot;
2. A plan or map of a piece of land.

Poser: A puzzling or baffling question. (Also: A person who poses.)

Raree:

1. A collection of things (goods or works of art, etc.) for public display; or

2. An unusual or amazing show or spectacle.

Sapor: Flavor.

Satori: The sudden enlightenment sought in Zen Buddhism.

Slew: A large number [of something].

Snit: A state of agitation.

Spoor: A track, trail scent, or droppings, especially of a wild animal.

Sri : Used as a title of respect when addressing or speaking of a distinguished (East) Indian.

Stint: An amount of work assigned.

Throe : A severe pang or spasm.

Throes: A condition of agonizing struggle or trouble.

Toot:
1. A short blast (as on a horn);
2. A drinking bout; spree.

Tryst: An agreement, as between lovers, to meet at a certain time and place.

Umbra: A shaded or dark area or part.

Adjectives

Acerb(ic): Acid in temper, mood, or tone.

Addled: Confused.

Agnate: Related on or descended from the father's, or male, side.

Agog: Full of keen anticipation or excitement; eager.

Alar: Resembling, containing, or composed of wings.

Alate: Having winglike extensions or parts; winged.

Anile: Of or resembling a doddering old woman; especially: senile.

Ansate: Having a handle or a part resembling a handle.

Apod: Without feet; footless.

Apodal: Having no limbs, feet, or footlike appendages.

Arcane: Known or understood by only a few; requiring secret or mysterious knowledge.

Arty/Artsy: Showily or pretentiously artistic.

Eldritch: Weird, eerie. (See: *outré*)

Enate:
1. Growing outward;
2. Related on the mother's side.

Enisle:
1. To make into an island;
2. To set apart from others, isolate.

Erose: Irregular, uneven; irregularly notched, toothed, or indented.

Facile:
1. Done or achieved with little effort or difficulty; easily accomplished;

2. Working, acting, or speaking with effortless ease and fluency; fluent;
3. Arrived at without due care, effort, or examination; superficial; shallow; simplistic;
4. Readily manifested and often lacking sincerity and depth.

Feral: Not domesticated; wild.

Het (up): Worked up emotionally by anger or excitement.

Hoary:
1. Gray or white as if with age;
2. Extremely old; ancient.

Inert:
1. Lacking the power to move;
2. Very slow to move or act; sluggish;
3. Lacking chemical or biological activity.

Lacrimose: Tearful.

Laic(al): Of or relating to the laity; secular.

Lupine: Characteristic of or resembling a wolf.

Opaline: Resembling opal.

Otiose:
1. Futile, ineffective;
2. Idle; lazy;
3. Useless; functionless.

Outré: Highly unconventional; eccentric or bizarre. (See: *eldritch*)

Ovate/Ovoid: Egg-shaped.

Repo: (Short for "repossession"). Of, relating to, or being in the business of repossessing property (as a car) from buyers who have defaulted on payments.

Retro: Relating to, reviving, or being in the fashions/styles of the past; fashionably old-fashioned.

Sere: Dried and withered.

Utile: Useful.

Wan: Unnaturally pale.

Adverbs

A pop: Apiece, each.

Amain: At full speed; with great haste. (See: *apace*)

Apace: At a rapid pace; swiftly. (See: *amain*)

Asea: In the direction of the sea.

Nigh:
1. Near;
2. Nearly; almost.

Supine: Lying on the back or with the face upward.

Amounts/Measurements/Weights

Are: 100 square meters.

Dyne: A unit of force.

Erg: A unit of force.

Gill: 5 fluid ounces.

Joule: A unit of work or energy.

Moh's Scale: A scale of hardness for minerals.

Ohm: A unit of electrical resistance.

Omer: An ancient unit of dry capacity.

Parsec: A unit of measure for interstellar space equal to 3.26 light-years.

Rad: A unit of energy absorbed from ionizing radiation.

Rem: A unit for measuring absorbed doses of radiation.

Sone: A subjective unit of loudness.

Stere : A unit of volume equal to one cubic meter.

Stone: A British unit equal to 14 pounds.

Tare: A deduction from gross weight made to allow for the weight of a container. (See: *tret*)

Tret:
1. An allowance to purchasers for waste;
2. Weight after the tare deducted. (See: *tare*)

Tun:

1. A large cask for liquids, especially wine;
2. A measure of liquid capacity, especially one equivalent to approximately 252 gallons.

Architecture/Arts/Crafts/ Decorations/Design/Makeup

Arras:

1. A wall hanging; a tapestry.
2. A curtain or wall hanging, especially one of Flemish origin.

Bijou: A small, exquisitely wrought jewel, ornamental piece, or trinket.

Cel: A transparent sheet of celluloid on which cartoons are drawn and then photographed in the process of making an animated film.

Dado: A rectangular groove cut into a board to make a joint.

Etagere: A piece of furniture with open shelves for small ornaments.

Eton collar: A large, stiff, white collar formerly worn by the students at Eton school.

Gesso: A preparation of plaster of Paris or gypsum and glue for use in painting or making bas-reliefs.

Henna:
1. A reddish-orange dyestuff prepared from the dried and ground leaves of the henna plant, used as a cosmetic dye and for coloring leather and fabrics;
2. A moderate or strong reddish brown to strong brown.

Imari: A kind of Japanese porcelain.

Istle: A strong fiber used for cordage or basketwork. (See: *oakum*)

Kiln: An oven or furnace for hardening, burning, or drying substances.

Oakum: Loose hemp or jute fiber, sometimes treated with tar, creosote, or asphalt, used chiefly for caulking seams in wooden ships and packing pipe joints. (See: *istle*)

Ogee: An S-shaped molding.

Orant: A praying or mourning figure in early Christian art.

Ormolu: Golden or gilded brass or bronze used to decorate or ornament furniture, moldings, architectural details, and jewelry.

Ovolo: A rounded convex molding.

Patina:
1. A thin greenish layer that forms naturally on copper or copper alloys, such as bronze, as a result of corrosion;
2. The sheen on any surface of something beautiful, especially with age or use;
3. A change in appearance produced by long-standing association, behavior, character, habit, practice, or use.

Plait: Pleat, i.e., a fold in a cloth made by doubling the material over on itself.

Pomade: A perfumed ointment, especially one used to groom the hair.

Sepia:

1. A dark brown ink or pigment;
2. A drawing or picture done in this pigment;
3. A photograph in a brown tint.

Serge: A durable twilled fabric of worsted or worsted and wool, often used for suits.

Stela: An upright stone or slab with an inscribed or sculptured surface, used as a monument or as a commemorative tablet in the face of a building.

Tole: A lacquered or enameled metalware, especially tinplate, usually gilded and elaborately painted, used in domestic and ornamental wares.

Awards

Clio(s): Awards given to reward creative excellence in advertising and design.

Edgar(s): Awards (named after Edgar Allan Poe) presented by the Mystery Writers of America.

Hugo(s): Awards given every year to the best fantasy or science fiction works of the previous year.

Obie(s): Short for "Off-Broadway Theater Awards," annual awards bestowed by *The Village Voice* newspaper to off-Broadway theater artists.

Tony(s): Awards for achievements in live American theater (primarily given to Broadway productions).

Calendar/Time

Adar: The sixth month of the religious year and the twelfth month of the civil year in the Hebrew calendar.

Aeon: See: *eon.*

Elul: The twelfth month of the religious year and the sixth month of the civil year in the Hebrew calendar.

Enero: Spanish for "January."

Eon:
1. An indefinitely long period of time; an age.
2. The longest division of geologic time, containing two or more eras.

Ete: The French word for "Summer."

Nisan: The first month of the religious year and the seventh month (eighth, in leap year) in the Hebrew calendar.

Stint: A length of time spent on a particular activity.

Tet: The Vietnamese New Year celebration.

Ultimo: In or of the month before the present one.

Agar: A gelatinous material (derived from certain marine algae) that is used as a base for bacterial culture media and as a stabilizer and thickener in many food products.

Alum: A crystallized sulfate/salt used in dyeing and various other industrial processes.

Attar: A fragrant, essential oil or perfume obtained from flowers.

Barre: A handrail fixed to a wall, as in a dance studio, used by ballet dancers as a support in certain exercises.

Censer: A vessel in which incense is burned, especially a covered incense burner swung on chains in religious services.

Dross:
1. Waste or impure matter;
2. The scum that forms on the surface of molten metal. (See: *lees*)

Elemi: A pale, yellow, oily resin.

Enol: An organic compound.

Ester: A fragrant organic compound.

Geode: A hollow, usually spheroid rock with crystals lining the inside wall.

Guar Gum: A water-soluble paste made from the seeds of the guar plant and used as a thickener and stabilizer in foods and pharmaceuticals.

Hoar(frost): Frozen dew that forms a white coating on a surface. (See: *rime*)

Ion: An atom or a group of atoms that has acquired a net (plus or minus) electric charge by gaining or losing one or more electrons.

Lac: A resinous secretion of the lac insect deposited on trees and used in making shellac.

Lath: A thin strip of wood or metal, usually nailed in rows to framing supports as a substructure for plaster, shingles, slates, or tiles (not to be confused with *lathe*).

Lees: Sediment settling during fermentation, especially in wine; dregs (not to be confused with *lees*). (See: *dross*)

Loam: Soil composed of a mixture of sand, clay, silt, and organic matter.

Loess: A buff-to-gray windblown deposit of fine-grained silt or clay (not to be confused with *lees*).

Macadam: Pavement made of layers of compacted broken stone, now usually bound with tar or asphalt.

Mother-of-Pearl/Nacre: The hard pearly iridescent substance forming the inner layer of a mollusk shell, used in decoration.

Muon: An elementary particle.

Musk: A greasy secretion with a powerful odor, produced in a glandular sac beneath the skin of the abdomen of the male musk deer and used in the manufacture of perfumes.

Nard: An aromatic ointment used in antiquity.

Nib:
1. A tapered point of a pen;
2. A sharp point or tip (also: A bird's beak or bill.)

Nide/Nidi: A nest.

Niter/Nitre: The mineral form of potassium nitrate, also known as saltpeter.

Paten:
1. A plate;
2. A thin disk of or resembling metal.

Peridot: A yellowish-green gem.

Recto: A right-hand page of a book or the front side of a leaf, on the other side of the *verso*.

Rime: A coating of ice, as on grass and trees, formed when extremely cold water droplets freeze almost instantly on a cold surface. (See: *hoar*)

Rood: A large, usually wooden crucifix.

Sard: A reddish-brown-orange chalcedony (a type of quartz).

Shard: A piece of broken pottery, especially one found in an archaeological dig.

Snell: A length of fine threadlike material that connects a fishhook to a heavier line.

Soie: A textile fiber of animal origin.

Stile: A set or series of steps for crossing a fence or wall.

Tenon: A projection on the end of a piece of wood shaped for insertion into a mortise to make a joint.

Urn:
1. A vase of varying size and shape, usually having a footed base or pedestal;
2. A closed metal vessel having a spigot and used for warming or serving tea or coffee.

Verso: A left-hand page of a book or the reverse side of a leaf, as opposed to the *recto*.

Alb: A long, white linen robe with tapered sleeves worn by a Christian priest at Mass.

Anorak: A heavy jacket with a hood; a parka.

Ascot: A broad neck scarf with wide square ends knotted so that its ends lay flat, one upon the other.

Boa: A long, fluffy scarf made of soft material, such as fur or feathers.

Calico:
1. A coarse, cheap, brightly printed cloth;
2. (Chiefly British) A plain, white cotton cloth, heavier than muslin.

Chador: A loose, usually black, robe worn by Muslim women that covers the body from head to toe and most of the face.

Clew: A ball of yarn or thread. (See: *skein*)

Cowl: The hood or hooded robe worn especially by a monk.

Damask: A fabric of cotton, linen, silk, wool, or synthetic fibers with a rich pattern formed by weaving.

Dhoti: A loincloth worn by Hindu men, especially in south India.

Fanon: A silk vestment with red and gold stripes worn by the pope. (See: *orale*)

Fedora: A soft felt hat.

Kepi: A cap with a flat, circular top and a visor (formerly the most common headwear in the French army).

Lisle:
1. A fine, smooth, tightly twisted cotton;
2. Fabric knitted of this thread, used especially for hosiery and underwear.

Miter/Mitre: The traditional liturgical headdress of a Christian bishop.

Mufti: Civilian dress, especially when worn by one who normally wears a uniform.

Obi: A wide sash worn with a kimono.

Orale: A Papal vestment. (See: *fanon*)

Ruff: A large, stiffly starched, frilled or pleated circular collar of lace or muslin worn in the late 16th and early 17th centuries.

Saree/Sari: The traditional outer garment worn by southern Asian women.

Shako: A tall, cylindrical military cap.

Skein: A length of thread or yarn wound in a loose, long coil. (See: *clew*)

Snood: A small netlike cap, hood, or hairnet worn by women to keep their hair in place.

Tabard: A tunic or capelike garment worn by a knight over his armor and emblazoned with his coat of arms.

Tatting:
1. A kind of handmade lace;
2. The act or art of making such lace. (Verb: tat)

Toile: A plain, sheer twill fabric, such as linen or cotton.

Tulle: A fine, often starched net of silk, rayon, or nylon, used especially for veils, tutus, or gowns.

Tutu: A short skirt worn by ballerinas.

Ulster: A loose, long overcoat made of heavy, rugged fabric and often belted.

Colors

Ashen/Ashy: Resembling ashes, especially in color; very pale.

Cerise: A deep to vivid purplish red.

Dun: An almost neutral slightly brownish gray to dull grayish brown.

Ebon: Black.

Ecru: A grayish to pale yellow or light grayish-yellowish brown; beige.

Ocher/Ochre: A moderate orange yellow, from moderate or deep orange to moderate or strong yellow.

Roan: Having a red, black, or brown coat thickly sprinkled with white or gray.

Sepia: A dark grayish yellow brown to dark or moderate olive brown.

Teal: A moderate or dark bluish green to greenish blue. (Also: A small short-necked dabbling river duck.)

Education

Academe/Academia: The academic environment, community, life, or world.

Con (verb):
1. Learn or commit to memory, memorize;
2. Study, peruse, or examine closely.

ElHi : Of, relating to, involving, or designed for use in grades 1 to 12.

Aioli: A rich sauce of crushed garlic, egg yolks, lemon juice, and olive oil.

Aspic: A clear jelly typically made of stock and gelatin and used as a glaze or garnish or to make a mold of meat, fish, or vegetables.

Baba: A leavened rum cake, usually made with raisins.

Cacao: The chocolate tree, or its seed.

Canapé: A cracker or a small, thin piece of bread or toast spread with cheese, meat, or relish and served as an appetizer.

Edam: A mild, yellow Dutch cheese, pressed into balls and usually covered with red wax.

Manioc: Cassava.

Mead: A fermented alcoholic beverage made of honey, water, and yeast.

Oleo: Margarine.

Olla:

1. A rounded earthenware pot or jar, used especially for cooking or for carrying water;
2. An olla podrida (a stew).

Ort: A small scrap of food left after a meal.

Shirr (verb): To cook (unshelled eggs) by baking until set.

Suet: The hard fatty tissues around the kidneys of cattle and sheep, used in cooking and for making tallow.

Taro: A widely cultivated tropical Asian plant used to make the Hawaiian dish, poi.

Til: Sesame.

Tref (adjective): Unclean and unfit for consumption, according to Jewish dietary law; not kosher.

Ugli: A large, sweet, juicy hybrid between tangerine and grapefruit having a thick wrinkled skin.

Ziti: Pasta in medium-sized, often ridged tubes.

Ankh: A cross shaped like a "T" with a loop at the top, used in ancient Egypt as a symbol of life.

Hadj/Hadji/Haj/Hajj/Hajji: A pilgrimage to Mecca made as a religious duty by Muslims.

Mene: One of the words in "the writing in the wall" in the Biblical book of Daniel.

Nae: "No" or "not" in Scottish.

Uomo: Italian word for "man," "human being."

French

Aout: The month of August.

Bon mot: A clever remark; witticism. (See: *mot*)

Coup:
1. A brilliantly executed stratagem; a triumph;
2. A sudden takeover of leadership or power (as in a coup d'état). (See: *éclat*)

Cri: "Cry" (used in the expression, "dernier cri," literally, "the last cry," but meaning, "the newest fashion").

Cru:
1. A vineyard or wine-producing region in France.
2. A grade or class of wine.

D'or: Golden; "of gold."

Eau: Water.

Eclat:
1. Great brilliance, as of performance or achievement; dazzling effect;
2. Brilliant or conspicuous success;
3. Great acclamation or applause; praise. (See: *coup*)

Ecole: School. (See: *lycee*)

Ecu: A French coin. (See: *sou*)

Eleve: Student.

Ennui: Listlessness and dissatisfaction resulting from lack of interest; boredom.

Entr'acte: (Literally: "Between the acts.") An intermission in a stage production.

Esprit: Liveliness of mind or spirit; sprightliness; high morale (as in *esprit de corps*).

Etat: State.

Ete: The season of summer.

Etoile: Star.

Etui: A small, usually ornamental case for holding articles such as needles.

Fête:
1. A festival, feast, or elaborate party;
2. An elaborate, often outdoor, entertainment.

Verb form:
1. To celebrate or honor with a festival, a feast, or an elaborate entertainment;
2. To pay honor to.

Fleur-de-Lis/Fleur-de-lys:
1. An iris;
2. A stylized three-petal iris flower, used as the armorial emblem of the kings of France.

Forte: One's strong point. (See: *métier*)

Gest(e):
1. A notable adventure or exploit;
2. A verse romance or tale.

Hautboy: An oboe.

"Honi soit qui mal y pense": "Shame upon him who thinks evil of it" (the motto of the English "Order of the Garter").

Ici: Here.

Idée: Idea.

Jeté: A kind of leap in ballet. (See: *plie*)

Lese-majesté: A crime or offense against a sovereign power.

Lui: "Him" or "her."

Lycée: A French public secondary school. (See: *ecole*)

Matin: Morning.

Matins: An early morning prayer.

Métier:
1. An occupation, a trade, or a profession;
2. Work or activity for which a person is particularly suited; one's specialty. (See: *forte*)

Midi:
1. Noon;
2. The Mediterranean region of south France.

Mlle: Abbreviation for "Mademoiselle," a term of address for an unmarried woman.

Mot: Word. (See: *bon mot*)

Nee: (Literally: "born.") Originally or formerly called. (Used to identify a woman by her maiden name.)

Plié: A ballet movement in which the knees are bent while the back is held straight. (See: *jeté*)

Raison d'etre: Reason or justification for being or existing.

Riant: Cheerful, mirthful.

Rue: Street.

Soiree: An evening party or reception.

Tasse: Cup.

Thé: Tea.

German

Eine: One.

Eis: Ice.

Essen: Eat.

Frau: Woman.

Gestalt: A configuration, structure, or pattern of elements so unified as a whole that its properties cannot be derived from a simple summation of its parts.

Ich: I.

Nie: Never.

Und: And.

Axel: A jump in figure skating. (See: *Lutz*)

Bocce: A game of Italian origin similar to lawn bowling.

Creel: A wicker basket, especially one used by anglers for carrying fish.

Ecarte: A card game.

Lutz: A jump in figure skating. (See: *Axel*)

Masse: A kind of billiards/pool shot.

Quoit(s):
1. A ring toss game;
2. One of the rings used in the game.

Roleo: A log-rolling competition.

Seed (verb): To arrange (the drawing for positions in a tournament) so that the more skilled contestants meet in the later rounds.

Taw: A large marble used for shooting in the game of marbles.

T-bar: A ski lift consisting of a bar suspended like an inverted T against which skiers lean while being towed uphill.

Tenace: A combination of two high cards of the same suit separated by two degrees, such as the king and jack of hearts, especially in a bridge or whist hand.

Trey: A card, die, or domino with three pips.

Greek/Latin

Ab ovo: (In Latin, literally: "from the egg.") From the beginning.

Acta: Actions, deeds, events.

Adeste Fideles: The Latin version of the song title, "O Come All Ye Faithful."

Ad rem: Thus, "to the point," without digression, relevant.

Aegis/Egis:
1. Protection;
2. Auspices; sponsorship.

Alae: Wings.

Amas/Amat/Amo: Three forms of the verb "love" in Latin.

Arma: Weapons.

Ars: Art, artwork.

Ave: A greeting: "Hail."

Dies Irae: (Literally: "Day of Wrath," i.e., Judgment Day.) A famous 13th-century Medieval Latin hymn used in the Mass for the dead.

Ecce: Behold. (Used in the phrase, "Ecce uomo" [Behold the man], from the Latin translation of what Pilate says in the Bible as he presents Jesus, crowned with thorns, to the crowd.)

Edile: In the Roman republic, an elected official, commissioner, magistrate.

Ennead: A group of nine.

Erat: Latin past tense of "be." (Used in the expression, "quod erat demonstrandum" [literally, "which was to be demonstrated"], often abbreviated as Q.E.D.)

Ergo: Therefore.

Esse: Is. (The present active infinitive of the Latin verb, "sum" [to be].)

Est: Is. (The third-person singular present indicative of the Latin verb, sum [to be].) (Used in the expression, "id est" [that is], which is often abbreviated as, "i.e.")

Et al: An abbreviation for et alii, et aliae, et alia, et alibi, or et alios, in all cases meaning "and others."

Et tu: And you, you too, even you. (Supposedly said by Julius Caesar—"Et tu, Brute"—after he was stabbed by Brutus.)

Eta: The seventh letter in the Greek alphabet.

Evoe: A Dionysian cry of excitement.

Hubris: Exaggerated or excessive pride or self-confidence (considered to be a "fatal flaw" in one's character) to the point of arrogance.

Ibid: Short for ibidem ("in the same place"), used in footnotes to refer to a source that has been previously cited.

Ichor: The "blood" of the gods.

Id est: "That is," which is often abbreviated as, "i.e."

In situ: In (its) natural or original position or place.

Inter alia: Among other things.

Iota:
1. The ninth letter of the Greek alphabet;
2. a very small amount.

Ipse Dixit: "He himself said it." (Used to emphasize that some assertion comes from some authority.)

Iter: A Roman road.

Kudos:
1. Honor, accolades;
2. Compliments, praise. (See: *paean*)

Nolo contendere: Literally translates from Lain into, "I do not wish to argue." (In law, it refers to a plea that means that the defendant does not admit to the charge but has no means to dispute it.)

Obiter dictum: In law, a statement or remark in a court's judgment that is not essential to the decision in the case.

Ora pro nobis: Pray for us.

Ovum (Plural: Ova): Egg.

Oyer and terminer: A legal commission that hears a case.

Paean:
1. A loud and joyous hymn or song of praise, thanksgiving, or triumph;
2. An enthusiastic expression of praise, such as a work of literature that praises its subject; tribute. (See: *kudos*)

Rara Avis: (Literally in Latin: "strange bird.") Something or someone that is abnormal, rare, or unique. (See: *sui generis*)

Res: Thing, matter, issue (used especially in legal contexts).

Sui generis: In a class of one's own; one of a kind; unique; peculiar. (See: *rara avis*)

Tau: A letter in the Greek alphabet.

Ursa: A female bear.

Health/Medical Care/Sickness

Ague: A fever marked by regular periods of chills and sweating.

DTs: Stands for "delirium tremens," an acute episode of delirium usually caused by withdrawal or abstinence from alcohol after habitual excessive drinking.

Ebola: A virus that can be deadly.

E. coli: One of the main species of bacteria living in the lower intestines of mammals.

Edema: A swelling of any organ or tissue due to accumulation of lymph fluid (or, in plants, of water).

Ipecac: An emetic used to induce vomiting.

Nostrum: A medicine whose efficacy is questionable and whose ingredients are usually kept secret.

Serum (Plural: Sera):

1. The clear yellowish fluid obtained upon separating whole blood into its solid and liquid components after it has been allowed to clot;
2. Blood serum from the tissues of immunized animals, containing antibodies and used to transfer immunity to another individual;
3. Watery fluid from animal tissue, such as that found in *edema*.

Stat: A term used in hospitals meaning without delay, at once.

Triage: A process for sorting injured people into groups based on their need for or likely benefit from immediate medical treatment.

Language/Printing/Speech

Cedilla: A mark placed beneath the letter *c* (as in the French word *garçon*) to indicate that the letter is to be pronounced *s*.

Dele: To remove, especially from printed or written matter; delete.

Elide (verb):
1. To omit or slur over (a syllable, for example) in pronunciation;
2. To strike out (something written).

Em: A measure equal to the width of a piece of type that is square or nearly square. (See: *en*)

En: A space equal to half the width of an *em*.

Erse: Scottish or Irish Gaelic.

Iamb: A kind of metrical foot in poetry.

Ode: A lyric poem of some length, usually of a serious or meditative nature.

Runes: Letters (associated with mystery and magic) formerly used to write Germanic languages.

Schwa: An unstressed neutral vowel sound.

Spondee: A metrical foot consisting of two long or stressed syllables.

Stet: Used in printing to indicate that a letter, word, or other matter marked for omission or correction is to be retained as is.

Tilde: A diacritical mark (~) placed over the letter *n* in Spanish to indicate a nasal sound [ny], as in *cañon,* or over a vowel in Portuguese to indicate nasalization.

Tome:
1. One of the books in a work of several volumes;
2. A book, especially a large or scholarly one.

Trope: A figure of speech using words in nonliteral ways, such as a metaphor.

Urdu: An Indo-Aryan language belonging to the Indo-European family of languages.

Legal

Banc: A bench or high seat of distinction or judgment.

Depone: To testify or declare under oath.

Estop: To legally bar, impede, or prohibit.

Ukase:
1. An authoritative order or decree; an edict;
2. A proclamation of a czar having the force of law in imperial Russia.

Machines/Tools/Utensils

Adze: A tool used for shaping wood.

Auger: A tool or threaded shank used for boring holes.

Awl: A pointed tool for making holes, as in wood or leather.

Besom: A bundle of twigs attached to a handle and used as a broom.

Cam: An eccentric or multiply-curved wheel mounted on a rotating shaft.

Etna: A gas burner used in laboratories.

Ewer: A pitcher, especially a decorative one.

Hasp: A metal fastener with a hinged slotted part that fits over a staple and is secured by a pin, bolt, or padlock.

Lathe: A machine for shaping a piece of material, such as wood or metal, by rotating it rapidly along its axis while pressing against a fixed cutting or abrading tool (not to be confused with *lath*).

Loupe: A small magnifying glass (usually set in an eyepiece) used by jewelers and horologists.

Miter: A surface cut at an angle to create a joint.

Oast: A kiln for drying hops or malt or drying and curing tobacco.

Piton: A metal spike fitted at one end with an eye for securing a rope and driven into rock or ice as a support in mountain climbing.

Tine: A prong on an implement such as a fork or pitchfork.

Dirk: A dagger.

Epee:
1. A fencing sword with a bowl-shaped guard and a long, narrow, fluted blade that has no cutting edge and tapers to a blunted point;
2. The art or sport of fencing with this sword.

Etape:
1. Supplies issued to troops on the march;
2. A public storehouse.

Gat: Slang term for a pistol.

Haft/Hilt: The handle of a tool or weapon.

Onager: An ancient and medieval stone-propelling catapult.

Sten: A submachine gun once used by the British.

Agio: A fee charged for exchanging currencies.

Baht: The basic unit of money in Thailand.

Ducat:
1. Any of various gold coins formerly used in certain European countries;
or
2. (slang) An admission ticket.

Ecu: Any of various old French coins. (See: *sou*)

Escudo: Formerly the basic monetary unit of Portugal.

Euro: The basic unit of currency in participating European Union countries.

Lek: The basic unit of money in Albania.

Obol: A silver coin used in ancient Greece.

Pelf: Wealth or riches, especially when dishonestly acquired.

Rial/Riyal: The basic unit of money in Qatar and Saudi Arabia.

Riel: The basic unit of money in Cambodia.

Sen: One hundredth of a Japanese yen.

Sop: A bribe.

Sou: A coin formerly used in France, worth a small amount. (See: *ecu*)

Specie: Coined money.

Music

A due: Intended as a duet; for two voices or instruments to play in unison.

Alla breve: A tempo marking that indicates a quick meter.

Ariose: Having a melody.

Arioso:
1. A style used in opera and oratorio;
2. A short vocal solo having the melodic style but not the form of an aria.

Assai: Very (in tempo directions).

Bis: Again; twice. (Used in music as a direction to repeat a passage.)

Coda: The concluding passage of a movement or composition.

Lay: An old name for a song, ballad, or poem.

Legato: A musical notation indicating that musical notes are to be played in a smooth, even style without any noticeable break between the notes.

Raga: A traditional type of Hindu music.

Rebec: A medieval stringed instrument.

Segue: A transition directly from one section or theme to another.

Ska: A style of music from Jamaica.

Sotto voce: Played in very soft tones.

Zydeco: Popular music of southern Louisiana that combines French dance melodies, elements of Caribbean music, and the blues.

Nautical Terms

Abeam: At right angles to the length of a ship or airplane.

Aft: At or near or toward the stern of a ship or tail of an airplane.

Alee: At, on, or toward the direction in which the wind is blowing (and thus sheltered from the wind).

Avast: (Used as a command.) Stop or desist.

Aviso: A small boat that carries orders or advice.

Belay: To secure or make fast (a rope, for example) by winding on a cleat or pin.

Davit: A small crane that projects over the side of a ship and is used to hoist boats, anchors, and cargo.

Dhow: A sailing vessel used along the coasts of the Indian Ocean.

Ensign (Ens.):
1. A commissioned rank in the U.S. Navy or Coast Guard that is below lieutenant junior grade;
2. One who holds this rank.

Halyard: (nautical term) A rope used to raise or lower a sail or a flag.

Ketch: A two-masted sailing vessel.

Neap: A less than average tide.

Orlop: The lowest deck of a ship, especially a warship.

Prau/Proa: A Malayan sailboat.

Prow: The forward part of a ship's hull; the bow.

Quay: A wharf or reinforced bank where ships are loaded or unloaded.

Seine: A large fishing net.

Spar: A wooden or metal pole, such as a boom, yard, or bowsprit, used to support sails and rigging. (See: *sprit*)

Sprit:
1. A pole that extends diagonally across a fore-and-aft sail from the lower part of the mast to the peak of the sail;
2. A *spar*, extending forward from the stem of a ship.

Thole (Pin): A wooden peg set in pairs in the gunwales of a boat to serve as an oarlock.

Archaic/Poetic Words

Anent: Regarding, concerning.

Anon:
1. At another time; later;
2. In a short time; soon.

E'en: Poetic abbreviation for "even."

E'er: Poetic abbreviation for "ever."

Enow: Enough.

Ere: Previous to; before.

Erst(while):

1. (As an adverb) In the past; at a former time; formerly;
2. (As an adjective) Former.

Eterne: Eternal.

Fata Morgana: A mirage. (See: *mare's nest*)

Fra: Used as a title for an Italian monk or friar; brother.

Ken/Purview:

1. Perception; understanding, comprehension, experience.
2. Range of vision, view; sight.

Mare's Nest:

1. A false discovery, illusion, or deliberate hoax;
2. A place, condition, or situation of great disorder or confusion. (See: *fata morgana*)

-ana: Indicates a collection of various materials that reflect the character of a person or place (as in "Americana").

-aroo: Creates informal or slangy variations of nouns. (See: *-eroo*)

-ase: Used in chemistry to indicate an enzyme.

Eno-: Wine. (See: *Oeno-*)

-eroo: Creates informal or slangy variations of nouns. (See: *-aroo*)

-ism: Indicates a distinctive doctrine, system, or theory. ("ism" can also be used by itself as a noun.)

-itis: Used in medical terminology to refer to an inflammation.

Myco-: Fungi.

Oeno-: Wine. (See: *Eno-*)

Oreo-: A hill or mountain.

-ose: Sugar.

Oste-: Bone.

-otic: The ear.

Proper Nouns

Aer Lingus: The national airline of Ireland.

Alero: An car model that used to be made by Oldsmobile.

Amana: A maker of consumer appliances.

Andrea Doria: A ship that sank in 1956.

Argo: The ship on which Jason and the Argonauts sailed in their quest to retrieve the Golden Fleece.

Ariane: A European space launch rocket.

Atra: A razor sold by the Gillette company.

Compleat Angler, The: A book on fishing written by Izaak Walton (1593–1683).

Edda: A folk tale of Norse mythology.

El Al: The national airline of Israel.

Elon University: A private liberal arts university in Elon, North Carolina.

Enola Gay: The bomber that carried and dropped the atomic bomb on Hiroshima in 1945.

Eri Tu: An aria from Verdi's *Un Ballo in Maschera*.

Eso Beso: A song ("That Kiss") sung by Paul Anka.

Esso: An international trade name used by Exxon Mobil, it was used in the U.S. before it was changed to Exxon.

Graf Spee: A World War I battleship.

Mir: A former Soviet spacecraft.

Nel Blu Dipinto di Blu: A popular Italian song of 1958.

Nehi: A soft drink brand first introduced in 1924.

Nola: Title of a song sung by Trini Lopez.

Reo: A "motor car company" (founded in 1904) named after its founder, Ransom E. Olds.

REO Speedwagon: A 1970s rock-and-roll band.

Sno-cat: A vehicle for use on snow.

Spode: An English manufacturer of pottery and porcelain.

Tao: A Chinese character meaning, "way," it refers to a principle or philosophy in Taoism or Confucianism.

Telstar: The first active communications satellite (launched in 1962).

Utne Reader: An alternative eclectic periodical that republishes articles that originally appeared elsewhere.

Spanish

Esa/Eso: That.

Fronton: An arena for *Jai Alai*.

Jai Alai: A sport from Spain popular in Florida.
(See: *fronton*)

Ojo: Eye.

Oro: Gold.

Reata/Riata: A lariat, lasso.

Transportation

Dray: A low, heavy cart without sides, used for
hauling things.

El: An elevated railway (especially the one that runs
in Chicago).

Semi: A tractor-trailer.

Ute: Short for a "sports utility vehicle."

Verbs of Communication

Asperse: To spread false or damaging charges or insinuations against.

Belie:
1. To show to be false;
2. To be counter to; contradict.

Cavil: To find fault unnecessarily; raise trivial objections; quibble about; detect petty flaws in.

Emote: To express emotion, especially in an excessive or theatrical manner.

Jape:
1. To joke or quip;
2. To make fun of.

Low: To utter the sound made by cattle; moo.

Mewl: To cry weakly; whimper.

Opine: To state as an opinion.

Prate: To talk idly and at length; chatter.

Pule: To whine; whimper.

Verbs of Motion/Movement

Alit: Past tense of "alight."

Gee: To turn to the right. (See: *haw, yaw*)

Haw: To turn to the left. (See: *gee, yaw*)

Hie: To go quickly; hasten.

Lam: To escape, as from prison. (Also used as a noun in the expression, "on the lam.")

Sashay:
1. To walk in an easy or casual manner;
2. To strut or flounce in a showy manner.

Slue:
1. To turn (something) on an axis; rotate;
2. To turn sharply; veer;
3. To turn or slide sideways or off course; skid.

Splay: To spread (the limbs, for example) out or apart, especially clumsily.

Yaw:

1. To swerve off course momentarily or temporarily;
2. To turn about the vertical axis;
3. To move unsteadily; weave. (See: *gee, haw*)

Verbs, Other

Abide:

1. To put up with; tolerate;
2. To wait patiently for;
3. To withstand;
4. To remain in a place;
5. To continue to be sure or firm; endure;
6. To dwell or sojourn.

Abrade: To wear down or rub away by friction; erode.

Abut:

1. To touch or end at one end or side;
2. To border upon or end at, be next to, lie adjacent to.

Ace:

1. To serve an ace against in racket games;
2. To hit an ace (one stroke) on a hole in golf;
3. To get the better of (someone);
4. To do well on (a test).

Addle: To muddle, confuse.

Augur:
1. To predict, especially from signs or omens; foretell;
2. To serve as an omen of; betoken.

Bedim: To make dim.

Deign: To condescend to give or grant.

Dun: To make persistent demands upon (a debtor) for payment.

Educe: To draw or bring out, elicit.

Efface: To rub or wipe out, erase.

Egest: To discharge or excrete from the body.

Eke out: To supplement with great effort.

Enisle: To set apart from others, isolate.

Ensile: To store (fodder) in a silo for preservation.

Enure: To come to accept something undesirable, especially by prolonged subjection to it.

Espy: To catch sight of (something distant, partially hidden, or obscure); glimpse.

Gird:
1. To encircle; surround;
2. To fasten or secure (clothing, for example) with a belt or band;
3. To prepare (oneself) for action.

Gnar: To snarl; growl.

Heft: To lift (something).

Ideate: To form an idea of, imagine, or conceive.

Inure: Alternate spelling of *enure*.

Lade: To load with, or as if with, cargo.

Lase: To shine (something) with laser light.

Lave: To wash.

Liase:
1. To establish liaison;
2. To act as a liaison officer.

Limn: To describe, depict, or outline.

Moil: To toil; to slave.

Opt: To make a choice or decision, especially, to make a choice in favor of something.

Peruse: To read or examine, typically with great care.

Rive: To break, rend, or tear apart.

Roil: To disturb, rile, stir up.

Rue: To feel regret, remorse, or sorrow (for).

Sate/Satiate:
1. To satisfy (an appetite or desire) fully;
2. To satisfy to excess.

Stint:
1. To restrict or limit, as in amount or number; be sparing with;
2. To subsist on a meager allowance; to be frugal.

Tope: To drink (liquor) habitually and excessively or to engage in such drinking.

Here are some tests, composed of crossword-type clues, to help you test your knowledge of the words in this book.

The answers can be found following the tests, beginning on page 184.

(The number of letters in each answer is noted in parentheses after each clue.)

Practice Test 1 (Easy)

1. If you do well on a test, you _____ it. (3)
2. Atom with an electric charge (3)
3. Vase (3)
4. "Therefore," in Latin (4)
5. Style of music from Jamaica (3)
6. Four slang terms for a "sailor" (3, 4, 4, 3)
7. Handsome youth loved by Aphrodite (6)
8. British actress, best known for appearing in the TV show, "The Avengers" (5, 4)
9. Hungarian inventor of a game cube (4, 5)
10. Mexican painter married to Diego Rivera (5, 5)
11. Something enclosed in a letter of enquiry (4)
12. Kimono sash (3)
13. "Motor car company" founded in 1904 (3)
14. Actor who won an Emmy for "Roots" (2, 5)
15. Zsa Zsa's sister (3, 5)
16. Two words that mean to "satisfy to excess" (4,7)
17. Young owl (5)
18. Racecourse southwest of London (5)
19. Latin abbreviation meaning "and others" (2, 2)
20. Large or scholarly book (4)
21. Legally bar, impede, or prohibit (5)
22. Suffix for sugar (3)
23. Encircle; surround (4)
24. Read or examine, typically with great care (6)
25. Somali supermodel (4)

Practice Test 2 (Easy)

1. *Ben-Hur* author (3, 7)
2. Male French friend (3)
3. Chief magistrate in medieval Venice (4)
4. Someone in an office "pool" (5)
5. Abbreviation found on a "wanted" poster (3)
6. Lacking chemical or biological activity (5)
7. "Chips" star (4, 7)
8. Gray wolf (4)
9. Jacob's twin brother (4)
10. Pooh's donkey friend (6)
11. Good man (Yiddish) (6)
12. Yale student (3)
13. Poetic word for "black" (4)
14. Rich Italian sauce (5)
15. Prefix for "bone" (4)
16. Spanish "eye"
17. Put up with (5)
18. Spenser (for hire) (6, 5)
19. Cremona violin-making family (5)
20. Bacterial culture medium (4)
21. Wood projection (5)
22. Figure skating jump (4)
23. Puzzling question (5)
24. Seventh Greek letter (3)
25. Poetry foot (4)

Practice Test 3 (Easy)

1. Fred's dancing sister (5)
2. Killer whale (4)
3. Dutch cheese (4)
4. Gillette razor (4)
5. Hurry (3)
6. Homer's outburst (3)
7. Gangster's gun (3)
8. One hundred of them make a yen (3)
9. Toward the stern (3)
10. Poetic word for "before" (3)
11. Israeli airline (2, 2)
12. Spanish gold (3)
13. Loop train (2)
14. Regret (3)
15. Welsh dog (5)
16. Brazilian soccer star (4)
17. Head top (4)
18. Popeye's baby (4, 3)
19. Seed exterior (4)
20. Fragrant organic compound (5)
21. A soft felt hat (6)
22. Former Soviet spacecraft (3)
23. Strut (6)
24. First Spanish month (5)
25. Munro pen name (4)

Practice Test 4 (Moderately Difficult)

1. Industrial district in Germany, the _____ Valley (4)
2. Fragrant oil obtained from flowers (5)
3. "Art" in Latin (3)
4. Sailing vessel of the Indian Ocean (4)
5. Louisiana music (6)
6. Head of a crime syndicate (4)
7. Hero of the *Aeneid* (6)
8. Melville's first novel (5)
9. Terrestrial phase of a newt (3)
10. Tech university in Troy (3)
11. English manufacturer of pottery and porcelain (5)
12. Statement of an amount owed (4)
13. Green layer on copper (6)
14. Perfumed hair ointment (6)
15. Imagine or conceive (6)
16. Fence steps (5)
17. Hawaiian goose (4)
18. Church hall (4)
19. Ghana capital (5)
20. "Hail" in Latin (3)
21. Suffix for an enzyme (3)
22. Irish airline (3, 6)
23. Lift (4)
24. "Brokeback" director (3, 3)
25. Japanese-American actor (4)

Practice Test 5 (Moderately Difficult)

1. *The Name of the Rose* author (7, 3)
2. Low man on the feudal totem pole (4)
3. People of northern Japan (4)
4. River between China and North Korea (4)
5. Nice season (3)
6. Early morning prayer (French) (6)
7. "The Rachel Papers" actress (4, 4)
8. English architect (1573–1652) (5, 5)
9. Adam's son (4)
10. Eye layer (4)
11. The "doll" in "A Doll's House" (4)
12. Styx Ferryman (5)
13. Expert (Yiddish) (5)
14. Ancient Scot (4)
15. Bishop's hat (5)
16. Grades 1 to 12 (4)
17. An eclectic periodical (4, 6)
18. Cattle call (3)
19. Disturb, rile, stir up (4)
20. French film director Jacques (4)
21. Olivia's acting cousin (6, 4)
22. Ossie's "Dee" girl (4)
23. Right-hand page of a book (5)
24. Unified pattern of elements (German) (7)
25. Radiant light (6)

Practice Test 6 (Moderately Difficult)

1. Tempest sprite (5)
2. Gossip columnist (4, 7)
3. Clam (6)
4. Walton's fishing guide (3, 8, 6)
5. European rocket (6)
6. Accusing French author (5, 4)
7. Venezuelan river (7)
8. In-flight announcement (3)
9. Hymn of praise (5)
10. Mysterious letters (5)
11. Jewelers lens (5)
12. First communications satellite (7)
13. Heavy cart (4)
14. Whimper (4)
15. *A Shot in the Dark* actress (4, 6)
16. Turtle shell (8)
17. African antelope (5)
18. "Rock and Roll" architect (1, 1, 3)
19. Met or Giant (4)
20. Adam's first? (6)
21. Uris hero (3, 3, 6)
22. Fonda beekeeper (4)
23. A ball of yarn (4)
24. Bible spy (5)
25. Mother-of-pearl (5)

Practice Test 7 (Difficult)

1. French actress who played *Une Femme* (5, 5)
2. Female British pianist (4, 4)
3. *Swept Away* director (4, 10)
4. Dance handrail (5)
5. Piece of fishing line (4)
6. "Behold" in Latin (4)
7. "Played in very soft tones" (5, 4)
8. Overdrink (4)
9. Dupe (4, 4)
10. Race of the Norse Gods (5)
11. "Saturday Night Live" actress (5, 5)
12. The first "Best Actor" (4, 8)
13. Young eel (5)
14. Russian-born French designer (4)
15. Large stiff collar (4)
16. A little grimace; pout (4)
17. Deduction of weight (4)
18. Pale yellow oily resin (5)
19. He played Ritchie Valens (4, 7)
20. Large South America rodent (6)
21. Guam capital (5)
22. Medieval Latin hymn (4, 4)
23. Describe, depict or outline (4)
24. Mrs. Cassavetes (4, 8)
25. Scottish ballet dancer and actress (5, 7)

Practice Test 8 (Difficult)

1. New Zealand author (5, 5)
2. Chinese nurse (4)
3. Ancient Greek noted for his loud voice (7)
4. Unusual or amazing show or spectacle (5)
5. Tearful (9)
6. Ancient unit of dry capacity (4)
7. What a theater producer prays for (5)
8. The "blood" of the gods (5)
9. Benson's cook portrayer (4, 7)
10. Insect in its final adult state (5)
11. Very young hare (7)
12. Mother of "Society's Child" (5, 3)
13. Wells race of the future (4)
14. Dickens band? (5, 4)
15. Hungarian actress (5, 6)
16. Polish silent film actress (4, 5)
17. '60s Tarzan (3, 3)
18. Resinous secretion (3)
19. Yellowish-green gem (7)
20. Thin disk (5)
21. Log-rolling competition (5)
22. Flavor (5)
23. Zen enlightenment (6)
24. Oboe (7)
25. Questionable medication (7)

Practice Test 9 (Difficult)

1. Asian ass (6)
2. Fish which is a "sucker" (6)
3. Flemish wall hanging (5)
4. Memorize (3)
5. Cassava (6)
6. Swerve (3)
7. "National Velvet" author (4, 7)
8. Greek goddess of the underworld (6)
9. WWII Intelligence Agency (3)
10. "ASAP" in an ER (4)
11. French letter mark (7)
12. Medieval stringed instrument (5)
13. Jai Alai arena (7)
14. "Odo" portrayer (4, 11)
15. Marine eel (6)
16. Long narrow fish (3)
17. Czech runner (4, 7)
18. "Usher" writer (abbr.) (3)
19. "Enigmatic" and "pompous" composer? (6, 7, 5)
20. Manor bailiff (5)
21. Bristle-like structure (6)
22. French army hat (4)
23. Samuel's mentor (3)
24. Silt deposit (5)
25. Former relief pitcher (4, 3)

Answers to Practice Test 1

1. Ace
2. Ion
3. Urn
4. Ergo
5. Ska
6. Gob, Salt, Swab, Tar
7. Adonis
8. Diana Rigg
9. Erno Rubik
10. Frida Kahlo
11. SASE ("Self-addressed stamped envelope")
12. Obi
13. Reo
14. Ed Asner
15. Eva Gabor
16. Sate/Satiate
17. Owlet
18. Ascot
19. Et al
20. Tome
21. Estop
22. -ose
23. Gird
24. Peruse
25. Iman

Answers to Practice Test 2

1. Lew Wallace
2. Ami
3. Doge
4. Steno
5. AKA
6. Inert
7. Erik Estrada
8. Lobo
9. Esau
10. Eeyore
11. Mensch
12. Eli
13. Ebon
14. Aioli
15. Oste-
16. Ojo
17. Abide
18. Robert Urich
19. Amati
20. Agar
21. Tenon
22. Axel
23. Poser
24. Eta
25. Iamb

Answers to Practice Test 3

1. Adele (Astaire)
2. Orca
3. Edam
4. Atra
5. Hie
6. D'oh
7. Gat
8. Sen
9. Aft
10. Ere
11. El Al
12. Oro
13. El (The elevated railway in Chicago)
14. Rue
15. Corgi
16. Pele
17. Pate
18. Swee' Pea
19. Aril
20. Ester
21. Fedora
22. Mir
23. Sashay
24. Enero
25. Saki

Answers to Practice Test 4

1. Ruhr
2. Attar
3. Ars
4. Dhow
5. Zydeco
6. Capo
7. Aeneas
8. Typee
9. Eft
10. RPI ("Rensselaer Polytechnic Institute"
11. Spode
12. Chit
13. Patina
14. Pomade
15. Ideate
16. Stile
17. Nene
18. Nave
19. Accra
20. Ave
21. –ase
22. Aer Lingus
23. Heft
24. Ang Lee
25. Mako

185

Answers to Practice Test 5

1. Umberto Eco
2. Esne
3. Ainu
4. Yalu
5. Ete
6. Matins
7. Ione Skye
8. Inigo Jones
9. Seth
10. Uvea
11. Nora
12. Charon
13. Maven
14. Pict
15. Miter/Mitre
16. ElHi
17. Utne Reader
18. Low
19. Roil
20. Tati
21. Maryam D'Abo
22. Ruby (Dee)
23. Recto
24. Gestalt
25. Nimbus

Answers to Practice Test 6

1. Ariel
2. Rona Barrett
3. Quahog
4. The Compleat Angler
5. Ariane
6. Emile Zola
7. Orinoco
8. ETA ("Estimated Time of Arrival")
9. Paean
10. Runes
11. Loupe
12. Telstar
13. Dray
14. Mewl
15. Elke Sommer
16. Carapace
17. Eland
18. I. M. Pei
19. NLer (National Leaguer)
20. Lilith
21. Ari Ben Canaan
22. Ulee
23. Clew
24. Caleb
25. Nacre

Answers to Practice Test 7

1. Anouk Aimée
2. Myra Hess
3. Lina Wertmüller
4. Barre
5. Snell
6. Ecce
7. Sotto Voce
8. Tope
9. Cat's Paw
10. Aesir
11. Cheri Oteri
12. Emil Jannings
13. Elver
14. Erté
15. Ruff
16. Moue
17. Tare
18. Elemi
19. Esai Morales
20. Nutria
21. Agana
22. Dies Irae
23. Limn
24. Gena Rowlands
25. Moira Shearer

Answers to Practice Test 8

1. Ngaio Marsh
2. Amah
3. Stentor
4. Raree
5. Lacrimose
6. Omer
7. Angel
8. Ichor
9. Inga Swenson
10. Imago
11. Leveret
12. Janis Ian
13. Eloi
14. Uriah Heep
15. Ilona Massey
16. Pola Negri
17. Ron Ely
18. Lac
19. Peridot
20. Paten
21. Roleo
22. Sapor
23. Satori
24. Hautboy
25. Nostrum

Answers to Practice Test 9

1. Onager
2. Remora
3. Arras
4. Con
5. Manioc
6. Yaw
7. Enid Bagnold
8. Hecate
9. OSS
10. Stat
11. Cedilla
12. Rebec
13. Fronton
14. Rene Auberjonois
15. Conger
16. Gar
17. Emil Zatopek
18. EAP (Edgar Allan Poe)
19. Edward William Elgar
20. Reeve
21. Arista
22. Kepi
23. Eli
24. Loess
25. Robb Nen

Richard Showstack is a freelance writer, author, ghost-writer, and editor in Southern California. He figures that he has done more than 10,000 crossword puzzles in his life, so he is familiar with all of the "cross weirds" (words that appear in crossword puzzles more often than in general conversation or the media). His other books include:

A HORSE NAMED PEGGY and Other Enchanting Character-building Stories For Smart Teenage Boys Who Want To Grow Up To Be Good Men

THE GIFT OF THE MAGIC and Other Enchanting Character-building Stories For Smart Teenage Girls Who Want To Grow Up To Be Strong Women

ePIFfunnies: Humorous Reflections, Insights And Musings on Life and Living

Son of ePIFfunnies: More Humorous Reflections, Insights And Musings on Life and Living

He also has a website: ePIFfunnies.com.

If you know of any entries that should be changed or words that should be added to *The Crossword Puzzler's Handbook,* please e-mail Richard at: rshowstack@aol.com

About Cider Mill Press
Book Publishers

Good ideas ripen with time. From seed to harvest, Cider Mill Press strives to bring fine reading, information, and entertainment together between the covers of its creatively crafted books. Our Cider Mill bears fruit twice a year, publishing a new crop of titles each spring and fall.

Visit us on the Web at
www.cidermillpress.com
or write to us at
12 Port Farm Road
Kennebunkport, Maine 04046

BOOK
PUBLISHERS